TRANSFORMING ADVERSITY
INTO
MOMENTUM

TRANSFORMING ADVERSITY INTO MOMENTUM

Ethan DeAbreu

Copyright © 2024 Ethan DeAbreu, All rights reserved.

No part of this publication may be reproduced, stored in a retrieval system or transmitted in any form or by any means, electronic, mechanical, photocopying, recording or otherwise, without prior permission of Halo Publishing International.

The views and opinions expressed in this book are those of the author and do not necessarily reflect the official policy or position of Halo Publishing International. Any content provided by our authors are of their opinion and are not intended to malign any religion, ethnic group, club, organization, company, individual or anyone or anything.

For permission requests, write to the publisher, addressed "Attention: Permissions Coordinator," at the address below.

Halo Publishing International
7550 WIH-10 #800, PMB 2069,
San Antonio, TX 78229

First Edition, June 2024
ISBN: 978-1-63765-607-5
Library of Congress Control Number: 2024908791

The information contained within this book is strictly for informational purposes. Unless otherwise indicated, all the names, characters, businesses, places, events and incidents in this book are either the product of the author's imagination or used in a fictitious manner. Any resemblance to actual persons, living or dead, or actual events is purely coincidental.

Halo Publishing International is a self-publishing company that publishes adult fiction and non-fiction, children's literature, self-help, spiritual, and faith-based books. We continually strive to help authors reach their publishing goals and provide many different services that help them do so. We do not publish books that are deemed to be politically, religiously, or socially disrespectful, or books that are sexually provocative, including erotica. Halo reserves the right to refuse publication of any manuscript if it is deemed not to be in line with our principles. Do you have a book idea you would like us to consider publishing? Please visit www.halopublishing.com for more information.

First and foremost, I dedicate this book to the love my life, Tsuki. You are the best dog a guy could ask for, and some nights, your silly antics were the only thing that brought me any happiness. I'm grateful to have spent the last year with you traveling, hiking mountains, and hanging out at the beach.

I also dedicate this book to my brothers, those by birth and those by choice.

Matthew, thank you for having my back this past year and helping me reach my dream. As your older brother, it will never be lost on me how much you have grown.

Also to the "The Crew": Andrew Desire, Andrew Lagredelle, Richie Mitchell, Vilo Lopez, and Nate Noncent.

Thank you boys for giving me some of your strength to lean on this year. You have taught me the true value of brotherhood and that I don't have to endure it all on my own. Especially Desire and Lag—you both called me almost every day this year and didn't hesitate to offer your help, even if I was too stubborn to ask for it.

Jeff Gao—as far as I'm concerned, we are blood, and our blood is 10% Hendrix. Kidding, and thank you for the amazing time we had in Spain and for bringing some fun back in my life.

Lastly, rest in peace Manny. I love you, and hope you find peace in your next life.

Contents

Chapter 1
The Road Ahead — 13

Chapter 2
From Cataclysm to Clarity — 39

Chapter 3
The Path of Serendipity — 55

Chapter 4
Flight of the Hawk — 73

Chapter 5
Frostbitten Dreams and Firelit Horizons — 89

Chapter 6
As the Midnight Frost Settles — 113

Chapter 7
A Steel Thread of Will — 139

Chapter 8
The Lastavica of Freedom — 167

Chapter 9
The Call of the Levanter — 197

Chapter 10
The Calling of Seeds   **219**

Chapter 11
Tranquilo   **237**

Chapter 12
The Art of Letting Go   **249**

Chapter 13
A Year of Sacrifice   **269**

The Whispers of the Soul
A Collection of Poems   **291**

   Clutter   292

   To Zero   293

   Growth   294

   Rooted in Love   295

   Thorns of Beauty   297

   Unyielding Resolve   298

   Threads of Light   299

   The Liberation of Tomorrow's Courage   300

   Unveiling of the True Self   301

   Embers of Transformation   302

   Venom   303

Omens	304
Forge of Ambition	305
Tempered Steel	306
Quiet Ways of Saying "I Love You"	307
Embracing the End of Suffering	308
Ethos in Action	309
The Illusion of Constraint	310
A Soul's Tempest	311
About the Author	**313**

Chapter 1
THE ROAD AHEAD

"Strength is a choice."
"There is no path to happiness, happiness is the path."

Every day, I question my existence.

What's the point in any of this? Why am I here? What should I be doing?

How strange it is to be sentient in this vibrant world around us. How strange it is to one day simply "wake up" and start experiencing and remembering life. None of us asked for this, yet here we are.

Is it a gift, or is it a curse?

When fierce bouts of cynicism consume me, I often consider that I am living in purgatory—a place between heaven and hell, my luck constantly balancing out with misfortune and vice versa. Sometimes it can feel that I always *almost* have exactly what I want in life. Then, right at the finish line, right at the precipice of the true actualization of my dreams, life just throws a hay-maker my way, knocking me down flat.

I've been on a bit of a losing streak lately. I got my ass kicked, my dog got her ass kicked, and even my car got her ass kicked. However, I am manually wired for optimism, so despite these rampant beatings, I'm here, still kicking. *Haha.*

However, even the most resilient souls have their breaking points. When my wife uttered those fateful words—"I want a divorce"—it felt like the ground beneath me gave way, shattering the life we had built together into a million irreparable pieces.

We had envisioned a future filled with love, laughter, and shared dreams—a life brimming with possibilities. But in an instant, those dreams were shattered, leaving behind a void of uncertainty and heartache.

In the aftermath of our breakup, I experienced a depth of despair I had never known before. Nights turned into endless cycles of tears, and the weight of grief threatened to suffocate me. Despite my attempts to maintain discipline and routine, even the simplest tasks felt insurmountable in the face of such overwhelming pain.

I just didn't see it coming. For about a week, my hopes and fears yo-yoed as she changed her mind between staying and going. "I love you more than anything, I want to stay," she said. Then I would say, "I never wanted you to leave, this is your home, our home, I love you." Then the next day it would be, "I can't do this anymore, I have to go."

When she would come back to me, my guard was up, and she could sense it. She would grow upset with me and plead with me to trust her when she said she was staying, and that I needed to trust her for this to work. Then I would lower my guard and open my heart to her again, just to get a slick uppercut to the aorta when she changed her mind. She did this about 5 times that week. It was only at the end of the week that she confronted me and said, "Ethan, we are getting a divorce, and you need to accept that! We are not separated, this is the end of us, so stop trying to win me back! There is no chance for us, we are done!"

At this point, I was completely burnt out and just said, "Okay, I understand, I can let you go." I calmly started throwing things away and putting away the things that I wasn't strong enough to let go of right away.

I decided to go on a walk around the community I lived in and called Andrew Lagredelle, one of my "brothers." Lag is part of a special friend group that we call "The Crew." The Crew consists of Andrew Desire, Richard Mitchell, Virgilio Lopez, Nate Noncent, Lag, and myself. Although we are not brothers in blood, we are brothers by choice, and honestly, that can mean more than blood at times.

I never allowed myself to rely on other people when I struggled emotionally. I never felt anyone truly cared, I thought people were only interested in gossip. I felt that all problems are better off being handled in-house, and discretely, but this time the weight of my burdens was just too much for me to carry. I was being crushed under the weight of depression.

Generally, I am an intensely disciplined person, and I am capable of powering through the worst of times and setting high standards for myself; however, this week was the hardest ones in my life. I couldn't sleep at night and would wake up with eyes welled with tears and a bed void of warmth. I couldn't bring myself to eat. I tried making my favorite foods to entice me to eat, but even that proved to be insufficient. I tried leaning into my discipline to give myself structure by starting 75 Days Hard by Andy Frisella of 1st Phorm, but when I looked at my wife, I just didn't have the strength. Every time I saw her face and knew that she was gone, it sapped my strength away. I felt weak. I felt my ambition and discipline inside of me, just out of my reach. Those positive feelings were just being smothered by the weight of it all.

I had no other choice—I needed the help of my brothers. In particular, I needed Lag, and I've known Desire the longest, so the two of them knew I wasn't okay. They would frequently check in with me and let me know that they were there for me and that I could lean on them. In my heartbreak, I learned to trust others again to help me when I fall. Most people who know me think of me as being a strong person, and they have this beautiful blind faith in me that I'm going to be alright. However, this time, I just couldn't do it alone.

As I went outside and spoke to Lag on the phone, I shared my grief and my ambition with him. I told him, "I won't let this destroy me. I'm going to make a plan, and I'm going to be okay." We spoke for about an hour, and he helped build my resolve. He helped me find the strength to persevere and let me know that all my brothers were here for me, and they had my back no matter what.

I went back upstairs with new confidence in tow. I have broken before, but I have always chosen strength. I always chose to persevere through the pain due to that pesky wiring for optimism. It is not easy to be an optimist, but it is necessary. Otherwise, you have nothing to hope for, and nothing can get better.

Upon going upstairs with my new resolve to move on with my life, my wife crumbled before me. "How could you throw those things out?! I wanted to stay! But now it is apparent that I cannot!" I was completely baffled. I was so confused that yet again she had suddenly changed her mind. I still loved her so much, and my newfound resolve crumbled away. We both cried, and for that night, she was mine again. My love returned to me, and I couldn't be more grateful. I even thanked God, and I am a nonbeliever. All my hope was gone, so I turned to faith for the first time in a long time.

Things were rocky but steadily improved over time. We felt more connected than we ever had in the past, and I was so grateful to have her. I was so grateful to feel life finally starting to make sense again, and I vowed to myself to pay more attention so I wouldn't get blindsided like this again. I had to protect the thing that was most precious to me: this life we created.

It took a little while, but after about a month or so, we were watching the sunset at the beach when she finally said to me, "Ethan I love you, I love you so much, and I am here. I want to be here with you. You are my home, you are my family. This life we have together is the most precious thing to me."

That meant something to me ...my eyes filled with tears. We had been working so hard on ourselves, and it felt like it all paid off, and all was going to be okay. I realized that every marriage has its rough patches, but what gets you through them is honoring the vows you made. You have to be steadfast. You had to be able to look at that other person and see more than just simple infatuation; you had to see deep love. A love that stands like an immovable mountain, unshakable, enduring, and permanent. She was my entire heart and soul. I gave all of what I was to her.

Then everything suddenly changed when the fire nation attacked....

She spoke to me in the third person and said:

"She loves you, just not in the way you want her to."

I was immediately overcome with a sense of defeat and loss. The impact didn't hit me as hard this time as it did a few months ago when she said it for the first time. When she told me that in May, it came as a shock, as I had felt that we always had a loving relationship. She was empathetic, compassionate, resilient, loyal, and intelligent. When I looked at her, all I ever thought was, "I want to share and do everything with you. You are the absolute love of my life. I would die for you, I would give all of myself to save you." Just a few days before, I had cute little text messages of how much we loved each other, silly jokes, and good times. I enjoyed the sweet little nothings that we shared, like the simple pleasures of having a morning cup of coffee together, making her breakfast, and going on walks. I never needed much to be happy; all I ever wanted was her company and affection.

All of that was over this time. We had definitively reached an end. I just didn't have the stamina to keep fighting. She wore me down, and I had burnt myself out completely trying to keep the fire alive. A few tears trailed from my eyes, but I accepted that she was gone.

For the first time in my life, I truly surrendered and accepted defeat. I wanted her to be happy, and if she couldn't do that with me, so be it.

I wish the break could have been amiable; however, she started lashing out at me and demanding me to leave our home, my home. She said she couldn't stand the sight of me, she didn't want to see me, talk to me, or even know I was in the same space as her. The fissure in my heart grew deeper with each passing word, second, and glance.

She left the house briefly to stay with a friend, and in the middle of the night, she would text me long rants demanding that I leave the house, telling me I was "despicable" and that she refused to co-inhabit with me. We never yelled at each other, attacked, or name-called each other, but she kept going for my throat, randomly attacking every insecurity of mine based on shared intimate knowledge. I was just so hurt and confused that she could treat me like this. I had friends telling me to "get my licks in or I'll regret it," but I just didn't have it in me. I loved her too much. If I came at her, it only would have hurt me more.

I was hoping that she would snap out of this bizarre mindset and realize that she was making a mistake as she had in the past, but this time there was no coming back. Her messages to me grew increasingly hostile, and when she returned to the house, she continued to demand that I leave.

I realized that the storm I was enduring was just emotional abuse. All I had in my heart for her was love, but apparently, all her love grew into malice. Under the immense pressure of the instability of my household and the workload of my new job, I realized that I had to get out of there ASAP. In a matter of a few days, I packed up all my belongings and threw most of my stuff in storage with the help of my one friend in Florida, Niklas Tessman. I was so grateful for his help. I steadied myself mentally to be prepared to do it all on my own with pure self-reliance, but then I drew on my new understanding that I didn't have to do it all alone. The loyalty and compassion he showed me by helping me out at one of the worst moments of my life will not be forgotten.

In a matter of hours, we managed to pack away years of my life into a 10-by-10 storage unit with space to spare. I treated him to lunch, said my farewells to my friend, and shared my hopes of meeting up again in the future. I went back "home" one last time and prepared myself to say goodbye to everything I ever loved.

I took one last walk around my community, soaking it all up with gratitude. I went upstairs, stood on my balcony, and took in the view of the intercoastal one last time. I said goodbye to my sweet cat, Orion, knowing that the fair thing to do was to leave him with her and for me to take our dog, Tsuki. I had come to love my dear Orion, aka Ori-no-kof Russian KGB Cat, aka Boyo. He was my sweet boy and the first cat I ever loved. I often dream about him, and I hope he is doing well. I gathered Tsuki and prepared to go out the door.

She came out of her room for the first time that week and wanted to say goodbye to me. I didn't want her to say anything to me, but here I was, drowning in pain, forced to look at her again. She said, "Bye," and I very awkwardly said, "Bye," without moving a step toward her. She lunged towards me, hugging me tight and hard. She stroked the back of my head, and anguish boiled in my mind. I was confused yet again, and I thought to myself,

"How can you hold me like this? How can you act as if you love me while telling me you hate me all week? Why is this happening? What could I have done differently? Is there a different reality where I saved us? Will she ever come back to me? What's life going to be like now?"

My heart swelled with pain as I felt my world fall in on me. She leaned in, and I thought she tried to kiss me on the lips. Utterly bewildered, I pulled away. She looked at me with sadness in her eyes, pulled me in, and kissed my forehead. I regretted hesitating and not kissing her back in the moment. I was just in too much pain to switch emotions from pain to love. I wasn't ready to let her go, but I had no choice. It was an out-of-body experience to look her in the eyes and just not seeing any love there. I felt hollow inside but kept reassuring myself that the only way out was forward.

I packed my car and grabbed the most treasured thing in the world I had left, Tsuki. My heart broke as I drove away. I had to accept my reality for what it was and have hope that it would all work out for the best.

I was fortunate that a good friend of mine, Kerri Brownell, offered me a place to stay as I figured out my next move. She was concerned for my overall well-being and tried to give me the breathing room I needed to get my head on straight. I laughed to myself and marveled at how a girl I met in the fifth grade at 10 years old is now helping me out as a 27-year-old man. You just never know how important the people you meet along the way are, I suppose.

I called my brother, my "brothers," and my mother on my drive to try and ease my mind as I went. Unfortunately, God or whatever beings at hand decided that this drive was not going to be smooth and needed to have its challenges. My car began violently shaking as I took it over 70 mph, and I just laughed to myself, because of course not even leaving could be simple. I pulled over to assess if there was anything wrong with my tires. Upon my initial inspection, I did not see any issues and continued along my drive with a one-track mind to reach my destination. When I drove at about 60 mph, the shaking was not as violent, so I decided to keep going. I just couldn't mentally afford to stop, and I needed to get away from that life. I wanted to just leave it behind so I could clean my slate and start fresh.

My phone calls raised my spirits and even made me laugh a little. In particular, my mother is always such a mom, always worrying about me too much. It can be frustrating at times; however, I can't blame her. If I had kids, it wouldn't matter how old they got—I'd always see them as my children. I suppose it was one shred of fortune in all of this mess that I didn't have kids. If we had kids, this would have been much harder. I never wanted to be a person who got a divorce, let alone a father that didn't get to see his kids every day.

My mom was more hurt than me to be honest, but I had to remind her to not say anything bad about my ex-wife because not even I spoke poorly of her. Hearing people say bad things about her certainly wasn't going to make me feel better. I still loved her, and I vowed never to speak poorly of someone I love. Our conversation shifted into her trying to coerce me into staying in a hotel for the night because truckers may be out to murder me if I used a rest stop. I rolled my eyes and told her, *"Hopefully they do off me."* As expected, she didn't find my response as funny as I did and continued to worry away.

Around 2 a.m., I started to lose steam and pulled over at a gas station in Georgia. I pulled the blankets out of the back seat and took Tsuki out of her carrier for a little snuggle and a nap. However, my mom's words anchored in my mind, and I was paranoid. One guy was lurking around my car while on a phone call that lasted too long for 2 a.m. I tried to convince myself it was all in my head, but alas, I could not. I started my car up again and hit the road once more, where I went for another hour before having to stop for real at a truck stop. It was pitch black at the rest stop with a few cars around. I decided to roll the dice, and I said to myself, "If I get murdered on top of a divorce, so be it. Clearly, fortune is not on my side in this life."

"*What are the odds?*" I joked.

I slept for about an hour and a half, then cracked open a can of Monster Energy and proceeded on my hajj to Mecca. Kerri was concerned that I hadn't arrived yet because I should have arrived by then; however, due to my decrease in speed and the function of time, velocity, and distance, I was not even close to my destination.

When I was about 200 miles out, my luck finally ran out. My car tire exploded on the highway, and I was forced to come to a stop. I managed to pull off on to an exit to begin working on my new set of problems for the hour. In the dead of night, I pulled off on a quiet country road. Again, I found myself thinking morbid thoughts: "*Ah, now this feels like the start of a* Wrong Turn *movie. I wonder if some incestuous cannibals are going to emerge from the backwoods and take me away?*" Half of me was paranoid, and the other half just wished someone would try me right now.

Do you know that graph? *"The more you fuck around, the more you are going to find out."* Well, I was at the outer limits of that graph.

As I exited the car to begin doing the devil's work in the darkness, it started to rain. In an entirely mentally exhausted state, I just started hysterically laughing and said, "Rain?! OH, WELL THANK YOU! I'm so grateful for this little shower while I work! How considerate of you to try and cool me off!"

After about 30 minutes or so, I was able to slap on the donut and start driving. I drove about 15 feet before I heard the random words of my brother echo in my head as I assessed why the car felt strange: "Yeah, you should always throw a donut on the back tire unless you want to die." My brother has a direct and matter-of-fact way of speaking. I could almost feel him rolling his eyes in shame at his older brother, who was clueless when it came to cars.

I sat still in my car for a second as I contemplated bashing my face into the steering wheel. I exited yet again! This time, I had to take my donut off the front tire, take a tire from the back, put it on the front, and then put the donut on the back tire. Fantastic.

By the time I was done playing musical tires, daylight had broken! I cynically thought to myself, "It's always darkest before dawn!"

This time, I was able to hit the road; however, I was now trapped in the new purgatory of driving 50 mph in a 70-mph zone. It felt ironic, and metaphorically, it was a huge practical joke that even though I was driving towards my destination, my ETA kept getting further away. I had 200 miles to go at 50 mph. Other cars zipped passed me as I reluctantly continued down the highway, a madman hellbent on reaching his new beginning.

The rain had finally subsided, so I rolled down my window and enjoyed the breeze as I cruised like a grandma in a Prius, invoking rage in all the other drivers. The drive was quite beautiful if I could remove myself from all the existential despair and suffering. I even saw a double rainbow break over one of the large fields on my left-hand side. I thought perhaps this was an omen of good fortune, but then I remembered the words of the Third Hokage and knew that it can also be an omen for snakes. Were these rainbows to indicate my future prosperity or further tribulations? Only time would tell.

I finally reached my destination by the afternoon. I hugged my friend and just sat down on the couch to breathe a little. She asked me how I was doing, and tears immediately welled in my eyes. I know Kerri well, and I know she is not the type to know what to do when someone cries, so I reeled it in and got ahold of myself. I can do all of that alone, in my own way and in my own time. I enjoyed a quiet Sunday before throwing myself yet again into another week of hell.

I'm an accountant, and the first week of any month is just utter torture. This job kind of threw me to the wolves as soon as I started. Fortunately, the position was remote, so that gave me mobility; however, my time freedom was extremely limited. We were pretty understaffed. Two people were out on maternity leave, and one quit the day I started. Normally, there is a bit of an acclimation period when you start a new job, but I was thrown right into the fire. I was working two jobs at once, so that made things even more fun. I'm a bit of a wolf myself, so when I gave notice to my old job, I knew that they would be in serious need of a replacement. My role was being made obsolete in the next few months due to automation, so it would have been a waste of time to train someone new to take over. It was a golden moment presented a golden opportunity, so I negotiated double pay at half the work time. It feels good when the little guy wins over greedy corporate America. Nevertheless, 16-hour days should take my mind off of things. I worked until about 11 p.m. every night just trying to keep up with the monsoon raging around me.

During the week, I also managed my time to start dealing with other problems as they arose. I had to get my car fixed, deal with some loose ends in Florida, and get my mental health straight. Unfortunately, this was no easy task to accomplish. My dog ended up getting sick because she became afflicted with fleas. Despite many baths, I was unable to completely eradicate them due to the scope of the infestation. Seeing my dog sick triggers a bit of PTSD in me from when my previous dog got sick.

Well, it is not so much seeing her sick—it reminds me of the day Fritz, my mini-schnauzer, passed away. He wasn't feeling well one day, so I stayed home from work to be with him. I was taking him to the vet in a few hours, but we never made it to the appointment. He was weak, and he didn't seem to have the strength to stand up.

In my logical mind, I understood what was coming when I saw him struggle to get to his feet, but it was too painful for my mind to process. I made him comfortable, tucked him in his bed, and pet him for a good, long while. I took some time to clean the house and played a Buddhist chant on the television to "clean the air" in a way. When I was done with cleaning, I sank into the couch to do some work on my laptop for my typical plethora of projects.

Suddenly, I heard him take a deep breath, and then his chest stopped rising. I rushed over to him and saw that he wasn't responsive. My heart ached, and I could feel panic trying to grab ahold of me, but I forced myself to slow down and think. I checked to see if any of his pathways were blocked and began to administer CPR to try and bring him back. I stayed calm and focused on technique and what I had learned. For a moment, it looked like he was starting to breathe, but then death pulled him right back into sleep.

In a panic, I looked for other solutions, other possible outcomes, anything I could do RIGHT NOW that would save him. I remembered that I had an epi-pen in my room, and I thought to myself that the epinephrine could jumpstart his heart. I made the steps towards my room...but I stopped myself. "No, this is too far." "What if you are wrong and only extend his suffering?" I clenched my fists and steadied my mind. I closed my eyes and forced myself to accept that my friend had passed. I looked at him, overwhelmed with grief.

I wanted to give him dignity. I carried him to the bathroom to bathe him and to clean his fur that had been stained in death. I wanted to honor my friend, his image, and his memory. We took him to get cremated, and I carried his body the whole way. I wrapped him with the blanket that always draped over us. He would sit in my lap cuddled up as I would work at my desk, writing my book, studying finance, and working on building a business. It was the most devastating loss I had ever experienced. Fritz was always my lifeline when we moved around as kids. There were times when he was my only friend in the world. He would sleep with me every night, and I would occasionally take him along on adventures while I did photography. He just soothed my weary soul and gave me the love I needed when I came home after a long day.

Tsuki, my shiba-inu, had such a sad look in her eyes. I could tell she was also stressed by the sudden change in environment, and I felt so bad. I saw her energy plummet, and my mind created scenarios of the worst possible outcomes. I already felt like I lost everything, but maybe there was more to lose and more suffering to face. The fleas were rampant and even infested my bed.

I was just so beaten down, with a broken heart, a stressed-out mind, and a body too depressed to move. Man, was my spirit being tested. Life just kept pressing harder and harder on me to try and break my will completely. I felt so disheveled and resentful. I couldn't believe that this was my life; it just didn't feel real to me. I was working myself to death, I felt abandoned by someone I thought was the love of my life, my poor dog was sick, and then I got sick from the stress of it all. There was just no mercy at all, no respite from the storm.

By Friday, I had reached a breaking point. I tried to get ahead of everything and started work at 6 a.m. so that I would be able to finish all my work on time. Unfortunately, I was assaulted with various other miscellaneous tasks throughout the day. The time kept encroaching in on me, and the pile of work ahead was still lurking there. Around 12 a.m., my spirit started to break. The frustration was starting to get to me, but I sucked the tears back into my eyeballs and kept pressing on. At 2 a.m., I hit another wave of exhaustion and wanted to give up. I just didn't understand how I still wasn't done. I was annoyed that I was not equipped to handle this close properly. I was furious that I was being crushed under the weight of work on top of everything else. Companies should really give some bereavement time for divorce, because I don't know how the hell I was functioning. I told myself, "Suck it up, get it done, just a little more. Not a soul cares. Get focused, if you concentrate, you can get through this in just another hour." I lied to myself.

At 3 a.m. I still wasn't done. It seemed like I had at least another two hours of work, and that was optimal. My spirit was at its outer limit when I saw my phone get a notification. I cynically thought to myself, "A light in the darkness? An angel encouraging me to keep going, and that everything will be okay?" Nope, just my ex. She decided that 3 a.m. was the time to launch her attack. Again, I found myself perplexed, confused, and hurt by her bizarre rantings. She was not apologizing or realizing that she loved me as I once had hoped she would. Instead, it was just a vulgar profession of hatred.

"Wonderful!" I thought to myself.

What hurt me more than anything was my inability to rationalize her hatred. I had done nothing to her, I was always faithful, I loved her deeply, and I always supported her.

To me, I knew that she was slipping further away into something else. The betrayal and abandonment I felt from her echoed in the broken chambers of my heart. I suppose this is why you shouldn't give all of yourself to another person—because it gives them too much power over you. She was the one weak spot in my guard. No one could break through the walls of fortitude in mind, but she had direct access to me. Every lashing was a direct strike to my heart.

I don't think many people understand how I feel, so try to imagine this. Every day for five years, you loved this one person. You both were affectionate and kind to one another. We'd have little spats here and there, but what couple doesn't? When we argued we NEVER resorted to vulgarity, name-calling, or anything of the sort. We would stumble in our approach to reconciliation, but that was more a product of being brought up differently. A mere two weeks ago, I had all these silly pictures and texts of us just goofing around with our normal antics. I had text messages with sweet little professions of love, and the "I miss you" texts when I was out running little errands. Just stupid, beautiful little things like that. Then all of a sudden, there is this burning hatred that seemingly sparked out of nowhere and was determined to completely incinerate me.

I questioned her assault and asked her to stop, but the tirade and tantrum continued. There is no rationalizing the irrational, so I turned my phone off and focused on a different beast instead: PSP Flux Analysis and Accruals, yay me. My vision grew blurry, my eyelids were growing heavy around 3:30 a.m. and I succumbed to sleep. I passed out at my desk after working 21 hours straight and woke up at 6 a.m. in a panic. I thought, *"Ah, getting fired would be the cherry on top of this hellish week. Perhaps this is a calling to cut all of my attachments so I can enter the void?"* My manager had picked up where I left off and completed my work. I texted her so I wouldn't panic over the weekend, as I was stressed about whether or not I would get fired. Her response was leveled, but I could see that although she wasn't happy, I was still okay.

I managed to survive one hellish week, and the weekend gave me a little time to start working on the thousand other things on my to-do list. I realized that although I was grateful for having a place to stay with my friend, it wasn't contributing to my mental health. I realized that I needed some time alone and that I needed to remove myself from the situation. I booked an Airbnb out in the country of McLeansville, NC, for some good ol' solitude. At the end of the day, if I have high-speed internet, I could live on Mars and still be okay. (Shoutout to Elon.)

As I checked into my new apartment, I could feel my cortisol levels decrease like little pressure valves in my head. The gauges had previously redlined and warned of impending explosion if things continued, but fortunately, the reactor was built on a strong foundation and endured.

I decided that I deserved a couple of days to myself, so I tried giving myself a long weekend to just catch my breath for the first time in a month. I was even going to try and grab dinner with a girl. Before I could do that, I was in desperate need of a haircut, because I felt wild and unkempt.

Apparently, it is wildly difficult to find a decent barber in NC; I went to several different shops, and nobody was taking me. As I left yet another barbershop, I encountered a brand-new problem in the shape of a Suburban. I saw a large Suburban truck quickly pull out behind me while I was stopped at a red light. I looked in my rearview mirror suspiciously. I saw a mother driving her children, and she seemed to be distracted. I thought to myself, "Please don't fucking hit me." Yet what the universe heard was, "Full send, let's put her in your back seat." The light turned green and I started to drive, and then WHAM, I had a truck hitched onto my Jetta.

I laughed maniacally to myself in the car, "Are you fucking serious?!"

My friends and I used to joke about how life will "hit you with a truck" when you are least expecting it. This proved to be true three years ago, when a Trailblazer rear-ended me because the kid was texting and driving. Funny enough, upon confronting that person, he was wearing a shirt that said, "certified genius." This occurred one day before my move and two weeks before my wedding, and it injured me for years to come. Needless to say, I was completely thrilled to be in the exact same scenario, with a bigger truck, after I had spent the last three years rehabbing my body. The pain in my back swelled, and I felt that beautiful tingly sensation of sciatica creeping down my leg.

We pulled over to the side, and the driver kept reassuring me that I was okay. I found this to be hilarious that she was *sooooo* in tune with *my* well-being. Then, completely not reading my boiling irritation at yet another careless driver fucking up my car and my body, she asked, "What were you going to do today?"

I told her, "The plan was to get a haircut, but that is apparently not happening." In an infuriatingly out-of-touch, southern hospitality way, she offered, "Well, I could book you an appointment somewhere, I know plenty of people!" Baffled, the New Yorker in me that wants nothing more than to mind my own business raged silently. I politely declined and said, "Bless your heart."

Okay, that last bit was a lie, I just thought it was funny. What I said was, "Are you being deadass right now?"

Okay that was a lie, too—I just said, "Thanks, I'm good."

I went to the hospital afterward and was in a good amount of pain. The professionals there were shockingly nice, which was something I have come to not expect from most healthcare providers. Unfortunately, their kindness was not equally met with competence. As I sat in pain for five hours waiting to do x-rays, knowing that I had no broken bones and that I more likely had muscle damage, my irritation grew. I was released with a prescription for muscle relaxers that I had to fill at my pharmacy...the next day! Because apparently, they couldn't fill it in-house. I was yet again baffled by the lack of common sense around me but limped on out of the hospital and found my way back to my car after an Uber ride. I drove myself home, crawled inside, snuggled my dog, and apologized to her for not just staying home with her.

There was just no respite from the constant maelstrom of misfortune brewing around me. I just wanted a second to catch my breath, but it was like being waterboarded by the universe. Every time I managed to gasp a breath of air, the world just continued to try and drown me.

My depression had been winning the battle, even though I had been putting up a good fight. It took every ounce of my resilience to keep pushing forward, but my discipline was failing me, and my job was just sapping me dry. I was working my first quarter-end close, and that entailed working seven days a week for 21 days straight, putting in 14–16 hour days as I learned how to do things for the first time. Needless to say, I was not happy about the situation. You see, I had expected "a weekend" during the quarter end, not every weekend in October. I reached a breaking point. I simply could not progress as I was.

My marriage had failed me, my body was failing me, my mind betrayed me, and all I had left was my spirit. A single wisp in me was waiting for its opportunity to burn. I turned my intention inward. I shut out the noise and opened my soul to the world. I realized being freed of my attachments was a form of ego death. The person that I once was, is no more. I needed to step into the newer version of myself and discover what that even looked like. I have always found some peace in mediation, but I just couldn't get myself there to focus. My concentration was scattered, and I was in survival mode. I needed to turn off those instincts, reduce the pressure I felt in my heart and mind, and find a center.

I closed my eyes and searched for the void within me. I let the blackness engulf me, and my thoughts evaporate off of me like mist. I embraced a state of total calm, and when the stormy waters of my mind eased, I was able to think clearly.

Our greatest obstacles are a calling to overcome them. Life will never dish out more than you can handle; you simply need to accept, adapt, and accelerate toward a new future. Sometimes it just might not make any sense at all, but it will in retrospect. When one door closes, many others can open. Love lost is just an opportunity to fall in love again. There is no loving others if you first cannot love yourself. You have to be able to appreciate the person that you are and wholly accept yourself before searching for acceptance in another person.

Then my mind would say, "But I still love her. I don't want her to be gone. What if she comes back to me? What if she regrets what she did? What if she needs you?"

"No."

I argued with myself.

"Do not hold out for hope—that is the same thing as praying for change. A hope or a prayer isn't going to change anything, Ethan. You need to focus on yourself. You need to accept that you are alone again and find peace and love in that."

My heart broke as I battled it with logic, but it needed to be done. I needed to put that thing on a leash again so that I could think clearly.

"She's gone, man, and she is never coming back. Let her go, don't hope, move forward. Savor this pain, raise your standards, and focus on your goals, and everything you seek will be yours. It is okay that you love her and loved her. That is not a bad thing, but now the both of you are different people, and that's just that. It's going to hurt."

"How long?"

"I have no idea, but you'll start thinking about her less and less until she is just a memory. Hopefully, it's one that you can look on fondly at times and see the good in rather than all the bad."

"I was so careful with who I shared my heart with, and yet I still failed. I loved her so much, and yet I still failed."

"It is okay though, you didn't fail her, no one failed anyone. She was just the first to let go, so now you need to let go, too."

I came out of meditation with tears streaming down my face. My heart ached, my mind hesitated, but my spirit burned.

We as human beings will face hardship, and oftentimes it will be life events that are out of our control. Life is long and filled with serendipity and entropy. The chaos and discovery of the unknown lurk in the future. However, we must stay true to ourselves in our hearts, and we must maintain our faith in ourselves and our resilience that at the end of the day, all you have is yourself. Anyone else who comes along has an expiration date, whether it be death, abandonment, or life just taking you in another direction, and that is okay. People come and go—they are just there for "the adventure so far," as my friend Niklas once remarked to me.

The road ahead is uncertain, but you should embrace the serendipity of life. You never know what gifts life planned for you. Every time you fall, there is an opportunity to pick yourself back up. Don't stay down; find the courage in your spirit to persevere when your mind and body fail you.

Chapter 2
From Cataclysm to Clarity

October 17, 2022

I've been contemplating loss, life, and rebirth. I've been burying myself in my work to distract myself from the droning heartache that rings in my chest. Quarter-end close was a good excuse to shut off my mind and just focus on trivial things like trial balances, reconciliations, and fx conversion fees. I was putting in 16-hour days just so I wouldn't have to think about any of it, especially my ex.

Work, once a refuge from emotional turmoil, now feels like a mundane chore. The days blur into one another, filled with spreadsheets and meetings, yet devoid of passion and purpose. It's as if I've been treading water, moving but not progressing.

Yet today my manager gave me the day off, and she said, "You've been working too hard, so please take tomorrow off." I honestly haven't had a better relationship with any manager before. She is fair and kind. When things were at the peak of uncertainty for me, she even offered me a place to stay, which truly caught me off guard because we had only known each other for about a month then. I'd like to think we have cultivated somewhat of a friendship. She offered me this day off as a gift, but it also opened the doors to thoughts I've held in check.

It looked like I survived quarter-end close long enough to begin battling that good ol' quarter-life crisis again. What happened to your "you are free" realization, Ethan? Do you feel free right now? What happened to your 'soul mate'? Is she still this radiant source of beauty and joy? What about your forgiveness—did you manage to rebuild the familial bridges burnt over the years?

Man, things never go quite as planned, do they? Just when you think you've got it all figured out, and that the stars aligned for you...the shooting star you wished on turns out to be a meteor that wipes all your hopes and dreams off the face of the earth.

Fortunately, I survived this cataclysmic mass extinction of everything "that was," and now all I'm left with is "what is." I lost my home, family, safety, love, and certainty. All the plans we had, the future we had discussed so many times, the dreams we held for one another, all gone in an instant. What's worse is that it couldn't be an amicable separation in honor of the love we once shared. Instead, it was a non-stop vicious attack on my character that was emotionally degrading. For one moment, she would speak of how much she used to love me and how sorry she was that things got so ugly; then, in the middle of the night, she would text me with very opposite feelings. It was a blind, thrashing hatred of a man that loved her with all his heart. Smashed to pieces, there I was, trying to just put myself back together again.

Work had been a somewhat decent distraction from the void that grew in my chest. Sixteen-hour days have the perk of making everything else not matter, but at the same time, the monopoly over my time grew frustrating at times. I'd have bursts of energy when I felt like myself again, and all I wanted to do was work on my projects, my writing, my photography, and my businesses. However, I would be unable to serve those urges under the weight of my duties. There simply was not enough time in the day, and I was not yet experienced enough to breeze through it all.

This day off was an unexpected respite from the last two months of hell. I knew immediately that I could not afford to waste it, and that today I had to take action for the salvation of my very soul. I had spent some time writing that morning, as I had been wanting to do the whole month. I immediately churned out 3 poems and started drafting the premise for my first fantasy book. I was in love with the process. Days before, my Nespresso Vertuo had arrived, so I was caffeinated and motivated to get things done. Stormio boost was my poison of choice, and the extra 20% of caffeine put some extra pep in my step. Caffeine has always done more for my happiness than alcohol, so I indulged, and I easily went through about four pods a day.

By noon, I realized that this week was the last week I was going to be in this Airbnb. I marveled at how fast the month had gone by and thought to myself how I regretted not going to see Hanging Rock. It was a popular hiking destination in North Carolina that has an amazing view of the mountainside. I was planning to go a few weeks ago, but instead, life hit me with one of those aforementioned proverbial—and in my case, literal—"trucks."

Then I thought to myself, "Why not today?"

I've always been a planner, and I'm not particularly spontaneous. I think it has to do with me being an introvert, as the idea of leaving my home, where I'm cozy and happy, isn't always that enticing. Even when I'm going out to see friends, I have to hype myself up for the drive ahead. I like to have time to think about something and get used to the idea before I pull the trigger.

When I saw the drive was an hour, I almost didn't go.

Do I really want to drive an hour to get there? That's kind of far, will it even be worth it?

"Come on, man, you love hiking, and you love mountain views. Grab your camera and go. You need to get back out there and do the things you love to do!" I argued with myself.

Nothing seemed fun anymore. My favorite food didn't taste right, my favorite games were boring, and I didn't have the fortitude to get myself to work out. I was just so tired. Every day I struggled to go to sleep and stay asleep. Sleeping was like the movie 50 First Dates, except when I would wake up, I would have to come to the realization that she was gone. She would find her way into my dreams, and it was always about some sort of reconciliation between us. We realized that this separation was a mistake, and that we should try harder to work on our problems, but the reality was starkly different. There was no reconciliation. Although I had logically let her go, I guess my subconscious was still fighting.

If you don't get the reference, congratulations, you have made me feel old.

I thought of one of my favorite quotes from one of my favorite books: "What is the most important step a man can take?"

"The next one," I thought to myself, completing the riddle.

Often times during the hero's journey, there is a part where the hero is defeated, his will is broken, and he knows he is needed, but he just isn't sure if he can do it anymore. In these moments, he turns to either melancholy or introspection. It would be all too easy for me to become a bitter cynic and critic of love and life. I can bemoan the cruelty and injustice of the world betraying my heart of love that I once treasured. I can withdraw from everyone and everything so that I may stew in thoughts of my misfortune.

I could just give up, but that's just not me.

My heart was waiting like a gas-lit stove. I could feel it clicking, trying to ignite from that spark, but I just couldn't hold the flame. I wanted it to ignite so badly, but it was just out of reach for me. I'm not sure if you have ever seen Avatar: The Last Airbender, but there is a part in the story where an old enemy becomes a new friend. He can bend the element of fire, generate it from within him, and manifest it around him. For years his spirit was fueled by the desire to restore his honor and capture his old enemy, but upon his reconciliation with the Avatar, he lost his ability to bend fire. He knew it was there inside of him, but he just couldn't connect with it. It was like losing a part of himself—the unique essence that made the most intimate parts of himself.

That's how I felt; depression, subtle as it is, smothered my fire. The discipline, tenacity, and ambition that raged inside of me were blocked. I was cut off from the source like there was a mental barrier around all of my strength. I kept walking the perimeter of this barrier, searching for an opening to no avail. I tried to force my hand through it, but I felt it devouring my mental stamina with each push. On this side of the barrier was death, and on the other was life.

I realized that my past methods were simply not working, and that the definition of insanity is "doing the same thing over and over again, expecting different results."

I sat down, closed my eyes, and resolved myself to go.

I grabbed my camera, a treat, and water, then hit the road. This was the start of my return to myself. I had to do this; now was the only opportunity I was going to have. If I hesitated, the moment would have been lost to time and duty.

The drive was quite pleasant. North Carolina is a pretty beautiful place. I enjoyed cruising through the back country roads. Great blue skies hung overhead and were streaked with clouds and jet streams. The sun was out, and it looked like it was going to be a lovely day. I felt my heart rate slow down, and a sense of calm washed over me as I took in the autumn's burnt fall foliage. There were trees painted in rich hues of red, yellow, orange, and green along the sides of the road. Perhaps their vibrancy can inspire some within me?

I finally arrived at the parking lot after driving for about an hour and making my way through the winding roads up to the overlook. I had driven 50 miles, and now the last couple of miles were up to me to trek on foot. I grabbed my camera bag, jacket, and sense of adventure as I embarked on my journey to the peak. I was poised and ready to capture even the slightest amount of movement in the tree line. When I do photography, my philosophy is to be quiet and slow. I expand my awareness of everything around me. I used my peripheral vision to spot movement in the corner of my eye and tuned my ears to hear even the slightest rustling in the bushes. When I'm focused, I can feel everything else fade away. I find myself present and seek my opportunity to seize, for just a moment, an instant, a glimpse of something beautiful as my camera shutters.

Surprisingly, there was little animal activity as I went along the trail, but many people. Something that I always liked about hiking is how kind people are. There is this mutual understanding between everyone on the path that we are all here to see something special that most people take for granted. There is a sense of excitement in the air and giddiness from those who have already reached the peak. It's one of the few rare times when you will feel someone root for you: "The view at the top is amazing," or "You are in for a treat!" These little exchanges lifted my spirits as I hiked towards the top in search of the fire of the gods, hoping to have what was lost restored to me.

On the way to the top, I picked up some little treasures. I found some quartzite and some other rocks with interesting patterns or a nice little shine to them. I always try to grab a little souvenir on these hikes so that I can remember them fondly as I sit at home working on projects or just contemplating life. They serve as a little reminder that adventure is always there for me, and I simply need to go if I feel called.

After about two hours of hiking, I finally reached the summit. I was nearly 2600 feet up above sea level and was just wowed by the majesty before me.

I made it, and I'm so glad I made it. I'm so grateful that I pushed myself to go, and now this view is all mine.

I walked to the edge of the cliff... and jumped.

Okay, I'm kidding again. I was checking if you were still paying attention.

The overlook was breathtaking, and I felt my heart melt as I took it all in. I felt all the other rocks I had been carrying on my back drop to the floor. The weight of this depression slowly lifted off of me. I sat down at the edge of the cliff, my feet dangling off the side. I let my mind off its leash and let it ruminate in little ponderings of big ideas.

I found myself thinking of my favorite book, The Alchemist by Paulo Coelho, as I steeped in thought. Every time I read that book, it makes me cry. I think that is because it is written in the universal language of the world. It speaks to the heart of things and what it means to be human, what it is to dream.

As the wind whispered and the sun shone down on me, I found myself imagining what it would be like to turn into the wind, right now, in this very moment. I wanted to reach into the soul of the universe and find the soul of God that exists in both the world and man. I wanted to alchemize and change my structure, to simply be free. I closed my eyes and spoke to the universe through my heart.

"Why did this happen? I thought I found her, that twin flame that stoked the fire in me."

The wind said to me, "I don't know bro, but you should go to the gym and get ripped."

I said, "Deadass?"

The wind said, "Deadass facts son, start banging and clanging E, forget about all those hoes."

I said, "Bet," and descended the mountain a wiser man.

It was clearly a northern wind speaking to me from NY and not quite the Levanter I was looking for. Although I appreciated the wisdom, I halted and realized that I needed to sit a little longer.

I asked the wind again, "Why?"

This time, a softer voice spoke and said, "I don't know, I am the wind. I simply am; I am shapeless, and blow wherever my whims take me. Perhaps you people are like me in this way. Perhaps you simply go in the flow of each other's currents until your whims take you in another direction?"

Perhaps you are right; a synchronicity is not supposed to be constant. It is more so a moment, an instance when two things align. We lost that synchronicity and, as a result, lost each other. Her winds raged, and rather than breathe life into my fire, she extinguished it. I tried to grow with her to be strong enough for her winds but was met with a hurricane. It was insurmountable, and I was being consumed by the black winds of Machin Shin. The wheel of time weaves as it wills destinies to be shaped or destroyed. There is always a purpose to life, suffering, and our reality.

I thanked the wind, and before he left, he mentioned that someone had been sending me kisses from the other side of the world.

Stunned, I thought to myself, "There is always another journey to be had. When one ends, it is so another can begin."

Then I spoke with the mountain, "What is the cost of your strength?" The mountain pondered the question, and slowly replied, "There is no cost, only time. As the times changed, so did I. I did not always stand as tall as I do now, but people always assume this is the way I have always been. 'Were you always this size?' they would ask. Of course not, you people grow from little seeds in your mother's womb. Then you sprout and grow into weirder little things. Some of you leave trash in my valleys, but some of you look at me and smile. Those are my favorite people."

"What changed you?" I asked.

The mountain said, "The will of the earth. At first, it felt like I was being destroyed. I used to be a flat field that spanned acres, but one day, the earth within me raged deep below the surface. I tried to keep the pressure inside, but I felt as if I was going to burst open. Before I knew it, I was sprouting into the sky, growing like one of you seedlings."

"Were you scared? You felt like you were imploding from the inside? Is it lonely standing so high?" I asked.

"Yes, I was very scared. I was just a humble field, and I never expected that the earth beneath me would burst!" the mountain said with a peal of booming laughter. "At first, I missed my acres

of fields; I felt so alone, standing far above all the animals that once grazed on my plain. I cried to myself and cursed my solitude. That was until the wind started speaking to me. The wind heard my cries and began to visit me from time to time, and he shared stories of the world he saw. The wind would always come with fascinating tales from around the world, and I grew to envy his freedom. One day I told him, "I wish I could be like you, friend. Your life is so exciting, and you get to see all of the world while I am stuck here. Your stories keep me entertained, and I feel lonely when you are gone."

"Do you know what the wind told me?" the mountain asked.

"What?" I said curiously.

The wind told me he envied me for having a home. The wind enjoyed traveling the world, but even in his travels, he too was lonely. Although he always had new stories, he found that fewer and fewer people were able to speak to him. The language of the universe was becoming a rarity among people. The wind used to love it when you silly seedlings would ask it questions or send messages, but you all have asked less and less. He told me that he envied that I was unshakable, that I was firmly planted in the ground, and that my valleys hosted so much life and abundance. He shared with me that he loved passing through my valleys, and he was always in awe of the animals, the trees, and the flowers. The wind loved breezing through the leaves in the trees that were always changing colors, and the sweet smell of the red maple trees. The wind shared that his truest desire was to be firmly planted in the ground like me, so that he would never be lonely again, and that for once he could create life and have the pleasure of watching it grow."

"Wow, that is amazing, the wind was just as lonely as you?" I said as I laid back on the cliffside. I rested my head on my camera backpack like a pillow and felt the cool stone beneath me, as well as the warm breeze enfolding me.

I closed my eyes and starting thinking to myself, "I suppose what they say is true, that destruction precedes creation. The mountain was just a field or a small valley until one day things suddenly changed. The wind changes as it travels in different directions and even has funny accents. I wonder if mountains have accents, too? Yet both the mountains and the wind, although they are both so beautiful and ethereal, can fail to see their beauty, and they get lonely. What's more than that, they are constantly growing and changing."

"Yes, everything is a matter of perspective. The wind taught me to appreciate my valleys and all the life that blooms in them, and I taught the wind to enjoy its freedom. The wind helps my valleys grow by carrying seeds in its winds. The wind even changes the very surface of my face each time he visits me. Yet now, I am not as lonely, because I have all this life happening around me, this marvelous view, and my dear friend visits me with new stories."

The mountain paused, and after a moment said,

"I realized that I was never really alone; there are just days when all I can think about is being a mountain, and not what it means to be a mountain."

"What does it mean to be a mountain?" I asked.

"To be a mountain means to grow under pressure. My insides felt like they were going to implode, I wasn't sure if I was going to live or die, but I endured because that is what good stone does. I exploded and broke, over and over again, but kept rising with these eruptions. I kept growing until the day came when I finally reached equilibrium. I was able to slow down. I am still growing, but just not as dramatically. It is all about patience and endurance, little seedling. I didn't know what was next, and I feared what was happening to me on the inside and if I would lose myself. In the end, everything was okay. The things that are uncertain can become certain again. I thought my destiny was to be a vast field for animals to graze, but it wasn't. I think it is a joke the universe likes to play on us. It leads us down this little path and lets us think that we have it all figured out, but at the last second, it changes our trajectory. To us mountains, the wind, and even you little seedlings, it seems arbitrary, but there is always a plan. All you need is the patience and endurance to grow as you are called to," the mountain said.

"You also need to have faith that you can grow from even the greatest disruptions to your life," I chimed in.

The mountain laughed deeply again, "You're starting to get it, seedling. Perhaps one day you will grow into a big oak tree, or perhaps a willow so that you can dance as the wind breezes through your branches! I will leave you to your thoughts, but do try to learn the language of the universe. I fear that my friend, the wind, is losing hope that others will speak to him."

Before I could reply, the mountain had grown silent.

I laid back thinking to myself and opened my eyes. Tears streamed down my face, and I let out a laugh. "Have patience and endure."

Sometimes, I forget just how small I am. I am a little seed being carried on the winds through this planet ...this universe. A small piece of cosmic dust gifted with sentience on this big spinning rock.

As the sun dips below the horizon, casting hues of orange and pink across the sky, I'm reminded of the fleeting nature of time. Each sunset serves as a poignant reminder to cherish the present moment, for tomorrow is never guaranteed.

I gazed at the mountainside, at the reds, oranges, yellows, and greens that splashed color into the valley. I looked at the mighty mountains that stood in the distance, and I had a better appreciation of their journey. I felt the winds wash my tears away and laughed as I thought that maybe even the tears that bled into the rocks beneath me could change the mountain ever so slightly.

Before leaving the mountain to begin my descent, I asked a kind stranger to take some photos for me. I threw my arms into the air and opened myself to the infinite possibilities ahead of me.

Everything was going to be okay, and despite carrying some of the rocks down the mountain with me that I took as little treasures, the load I was carrying felt lighter.

I'm never really alone; if I want company, I just need to speak in the language of the universe. The mountains, the winds, the sun, the moon, the seas, and more are all there for me to speak with. At the end of the day, I guess we can all feel a little lonely from time to time, but the only way to cure that loneliness is to keep an open heart.

I left my burdens behind, and I left with a vow: "I will learn the language of the universe so I can cure the lonely hearts that have forgotten the language. I'll be a little seed that can bring about new life."

Chapter 3
THE PATH OF SERENDIPITY

October 27, 2022

Today I wasn't sure what I was thinking about. I had been trying to start these hikes with an intention or a quote to think about, but today, I was going with a freestyle.

The quarter-end accounting close was basically over, and my team had a "work hard, play hard" policy. Technically I have "unlimited" PTO, so why be afraid to take a few days? One cool benefit from my company is that I get the last Friday of every month off as a "Global Refresh Day." That was a mini-manifestation for me, because I always said if I employed people one day, I would do the same. I think it is just good leadership to give back to your employees after you take from them. I had been working 16-hour days, seven days a week, for the entire month. I was in desperate need of a break, so I took one additional day off to give myself a four-day weekend.

Although only 10 days had passed since I hiked Hanging Rock, I found myself in a new home in a different state. Currently, I was staying in Roanoke Virginia with my little Tsuki. This was all intentional, of course, as I had set the goal of hiking McAfee Knob, a beautiful overlook that is part of Virginia's "Triple Crown." Perhaps one day I will hike all three, but for today, it was good ol' McAfee. It is apparently on most hikers' bucket lists and is generally a little crowded on the weekends. Having the foresight of this knowledge, I decided Thursday morning was the best time for my hike. I wanted to get there early to ensure that I got parking because I heard that was problematic.

Perched atop Catawba Mountain at approximately 3,200 feet, McAfee Knob promises a breathtaking 270-degree panoramic view. Anticipating a six-hour round-trip hike, I opted to leave Tsuki behind, deeming the trail too rigorous for her.

My alarm sounded at 7 a.m. and I crawled out of bed. I started to collect myself for the hike, and I brewed a nice cup of Stormio Boost Nespresso to wake myself up a little before heading out. Then I grabbed my camera bag, jacket, and water, kissed my pup goodbye, and was out the door.

I took about ten steps before I heard a pitiful little cry from my apartment: "BoooooooooooWooooooooooooo." The little yodel of Tsuki could be heard by everyone in the complex, and I felt so bad leaving her behind. She developed a little bit of anxiety from the divorce. She misses her mom, and I'm sure she misses sitting out on our balcony in Fort Lauderdale. As a matter of fact, she used to demand to be let out on the balcony first thing every morning. As soon as she heard me stir awake in bed, I would listen to her trot to the sliding door, do her stretch, and claw against the metal of the door.

I always got a kick out of her doing that, then I would crawl out of bed and open the door for her to bask in the sun and warm beach breeze. As she went outside, I would grab my "boyo," Orion, and give him a snuggle until Tsuki got jealous and circled back to drag me outside, too.

Now all of that was just a distant memory—one that wasn't as distant as I would like it to be. I took about two more steps away, thinking to myself, "She needs to stay here, the hike is too intense for her, and she needs to figure out how to be okay hanging out at home again."

Then another whine sounded even louder: "BOOOOWOOOOOWOOOOO."

I slumped my shoulders, sighed, and returned to my apartment. I opened the door, and there she was in full-blown wiggles, so excited to see me again after I left for a total of two minutes. She nibbled my hand to demand more pets from me. I crouched down, scooped her up like a baby, and said, "Bub, I already told you, I would never abandon you. When I leave, I will always come back for you." Then I hit her with the multi-kiss combo, which makes her beam with a smile.

I looked at her, then I looked at the door and said, "Screw it."

I threw on her angel wing harness, grabbed some treats, and packed her up with me. Once we got to the car, I put her in the carrier so she would be safer than just running amok in my car. I even put her seatbelt on, just to be extra safe.

I spoke to her softly as she got settled. She was just happy to be with me, "Okay, from now on, where I go, you go. When you get tired of walking, I'll carry you around in the backpack, deal?"

I rolled my eyes as I saw the smile in hers, "You have no idea what I'm saying, but you are so good at negotiating! Good job holding your ground. You got what you wanted, but I hope you are ready for a long walk today. Just do me one favor, okay? Please don't run off a cliff, and if a bobcat or bear comes around, just let Dad handle it, okay? I know you think you're tough, but trust me, let me handle it."

After a short drive, we reached the mountain, and there was ample parking since it was a Thursday. I started to get situated, and I compromised on bringing my camera bag so that I could bring her carrier for when she inevitably got tired, but I managed to squeeze a water bottle, a whiskey bottle, and a shot glass into the bag, as I committed to just wearing my camera around my neck the way up. I also looped my tripod onto the backpack carrier.

We had to cross the street to get to the trail, so I decided it would be best to carry her. I scooped her up and jogged across. There was a small gate blocking the trail, so I simply hopped over with Tsuki in tow.

The fall foliage was in true abundance, and a rainbow of leaves was scattered across the trail. The breeze was nice and comforting, and the smell of morning dew filled my nose and lungs. There is always an immediate feeling of relief when

I take that first intentional breath of air. I imagine that is how cigarette smokers must feel when they take their first drag. It's like a cool rush of air that you can feel circulate throughout your entire body, a wave of peace that washes over all the stress. Finally, just able to *breathe*.

It took me a minute to get accustomed to having Tsuki with me because I was used to and fond of the solitude of these hikes. I like embracing the silence, no words spoken, and just slowly walking to my inevitable destination. I keep an ethos of being "fully integrated" in nature, inspired by the book *For Whom the Bell Tolls*.

When you slow down, you start to notice all the things that you would normally miss.

In my paranoia, I would frequently mistake the crunching of leaves around me for bears when it was just squirrels being little trolls tromping around. There was a video that went viral recently of a hiker who got attacked by a bear on a trail and successfully fended it off. That made bears come to the forefront of my mind while on these hikes. If you aren't familiar with my luck, please refer to the previous chapters, and then we can decide if I'm being melodramatic or not. I really should get some bear mace, just in case.

A good friend of mine named Vin has this terrible fear of bears. He once sent me a Snapchat of him freaking out in the woods because he thought he heard one and ran back to his friend's house. It was hysterical, and we all would relentlessly tease him about his fear of bears. He would always hold his ground and say, "They are terrifying killing machines. Who wouldn't be scared?" We would all laugh and not take him seriously; however, Karma is a bitch, and I know my clock is ticking down to a bear encounter. I might as well be prepared for it when my day comes, so Vin can make fun of me and say, "I told you so."

I let my paranoia slide to the back of my mind and instead focused on the occasional *scream* of a blue jay. They have such awful chirps that scrape on my mental blackboard. However, I learned recently that most times when a blue jay jeers, it is a sign of its distress over there being a hawk in the area. Although their scream is annoying, it is a clever adaptation, as they are trying to mimic the cry of a red-shouldered hawk to scare them off from their area. They also scream to court the lady jays, so I suppose I can't fault them for using the analog version of Twitter to send out news and let the ladies know they are available. Most people do the same thing; we are always screaming our completely unsolicited opinions out into the void in hopes that someone agrees or validates what we are saying. I guess I'm no different!

After walking the trail for about an hour and a half, I was surprised at the lack of wildlife. Squirrels were abundant; however, I always go on these walks in hopes of seeing something truly beautiful or unique. I was becoming a little disappointed that I had not seen anything, and I thought perhaps Tsuki may have been scaring away the other animals, because she would rabidly assault any leaf that blew in the wind. Then I realized that all I had to do was slow down even more.

Once again, I tried to get my mind back on track. I was certainly ruminating, but they were not quite the ruminations that are quintessential to personal development that I am hoping to inspire. I closed my eyes, paused, and took another deep breath in. I could smell the faintest hint of mountain mint in the air. I have always found the fragrance of mint to be soothing, so I thanked the mountain for trying to ease my spirit.

As I stood in place quietly, I started to tune my hearing into the environment around me. I heard more crunching leaves, some pecking on the trees, and the sounds of birds chirping. A smile bloomed on my face as I realized that what I was looking for was all around me the entire time, and all I had to do was give it time to present itself. Sometimes the treasures that we seek are right under our noses.

Life itself is a journey to an inevitable destination, yet so many of us fail to stop and take in the scenery. I hope reincarnation is real, because I'm only 27 now, and I know that I would like to do this all over again, in a different way and at a different time. I often look back on my life and think about the things I would have done differently had I known what I know today. I don't do this in a way drenched in melancholy or regret, but just as a little pondering of what could have been.

Perhaps if I could have done things differently, I would have loved to have studied at Princeton University. Perhaps I would have studied marketing instead of accounting, and photography as well. Princeton has the most beautiful campus—it looks like it is straight out of one of my favorite books, *The Name of the Wind*. I felt like a young Kvothe walking through the grandiose campus when I was with *her*....

Ah, there it is, the block to deeper thoughts. I just can't escape the thought of you.

That makes her my Denna. Although book three has yet to come...

Seriously, Rothfuss, crank that book out man! We are all dying here waiting for you!

...I already know she is the one that will break Kvothe. We are told from the beginning that Kvothe is not sharing a hero's story, but rather a tragedy. He falls in love with Denna throughout the book, and it seems like it is a beautiful romance, but that was all intentional. You are slowly being lured into a sense of safety, and you may have even been rooting for their love. All of it would have been naïve, though; you were being set up for failure, and you didn't even know. The one thing that can destroy a man is love. The words haven't been written yet, but Denna will absolutely be the one to break this man. In Kvothe's despair, he has lost his inner strength and his ability to use "sympathy" (magic-ish). Even in the moments when it was a matter of life and death, he just could not summon the "magic" forward. He had lost his connection to it.

In some ways, I feel like an older Kvothe. I have a relentlessly curious mind, but that curiosity can get me in trouble. I was too taken in by her, curious about what kind of life we could live together, but in doing so, I exposed myself to critical damage. Love is just about the craziest and most irrational thing you can do. To completely give yourself to another person means you risk losing yourself. We are little dopamine fiends that are willing to pay any price to be loved. We become addicted to the feeling, and we give away more and more of ourselves until we are emotionally destitute and have to file for bankruptcy.

The depression I felt came in waves. I felt like all my motivations were just out of reach. I'd have little surges of productivity and feel that everything was going to be okay, but then as the day drew to a close, that feeling would sink back in. It was like a forcefield that I could feel blocking the connection between my mind and my heart. My brain was doing everything possible to shield me from the pain, and my heart just rampaged against its confinement. Although it was boxed up inside of me, I also seemed to lock away my passion and drive with it. I'm still struggling to get my workouts in and to just have clarity; however, each day is a little easier. I've been meditating daily for about 10 minutes a day just to try and connect with that fire inside of me. I feel like an engine that keeps cranking but won't start. I haven't completely worked out how to fix the problem. Every time I do one repair and think I'm good to go, there always turns out to be another light on my dashboard. I'd get my engine to turn over from time to time but would come to realize that I was nearly out of gas or my tire pressure was too low.

I abandoned myself, and now, this is the punishment.

However, today is a new day and another opportunity to try and ignite that fire inside of me again. Perhaps like Prometheus, I can steal a bolt of lightning from the top of the mountain. I think that's why I feel drawn to the mountains and nature now. I'm searching for that fire, I'm trying to talk with God, and I need to face myself. There is just something so inspiring about mountains—I think that is what draws us in. In many stories of the "hero's journey," there is a part where they have to climb a mountain in search of truth.

Two of my favorite examples of this are in *The Wheel of Time* and *Avatar: The Last Airbender*. The characters would find themselves in a place of ego death or feeling lost but would devote all their energy to overcoming this mountain. We are all going to have moments in life where we are going to face a mountain.

Tsuki and I hiked for about four hours to the top of McAffee Knob. Lost in contemplation, I reflected on life's journey, pondering the roads not taken and the lessons learned. As memories of past regrets mingled with hopes for the future, I found solace in the boundless expanse of the wilderness.

Upon reaching the summit of McAfee Knob, I basked in the awe-inspiring vista, grateful for the respite from the confines of routine. With each breath of mountain air, I felt a resurgence of vitality, a flicker of passion reigniting within me. The trees were charred with autumn's burn, and the sky was full and bright. It was such a vivid contrast to the two-dimensional world of Microsoft Excel I was living in. Two-dimensional thinking has the benefit of removing that layer of complexity, but it is just a boring world of no-good solutions. It has quick fixes for powering through but not a satisfying solution.

I thanked the trail for the challenge, the rocks that made me slip and fall along the way, Tsuki for giving me company to the top, and the cool breeze at the top for refreshing me. I took off my leather jacket that clung to my skin with sweat, and I closed my eyes. I laughed and took a deep breath in. It was more than the fresh mountain air; it was a breath of freedom, rebellion, and inspiration! In my heart, I felt the wind pass through each chamber, cleaning out the ash of what was once there. It was giving a breath of life to the ember that dared to keep smoldering.

It is a burning inferno inside of me that demands more. Every time I have failed, I learned from that man and laid him to rest as I climbed back up the mountain a newer version of myself. I have to reach deep within myself to find purpose, and once I understand what I truly desire again, I can figure out the "how."

I opened my eyes again and smiled to myself. I could feel myself healing, and I could feel my passion coming back to me. The forcefield grew weaker, and I could feel my "broken" heart still beating, still curious, and still determined.

Feeling a little silly, Tsuki and I recreated the iconic cover of *The Lion King* as I held her up overhead, angel wing harness on, and presented her to all of Mcaffee Knob.

"Everything the light touches is our kingdom."

Tsuki, as always, trusted everything I said but already knew the world was hers. She's so spoiled.

I noticed that there was quite a bit more to the cliffside than just the knob, so I decided to keep walking down the path to see what other views there may be. I found a nice quiet spot by a ledge where I could hear my thoughts a little more clearly.

I drew the bottle of Heaven's Door whiskey my Uncle Nick gifted me from the bag, as well as a shot glass from Joshua Tree that was also a gift. I poured a shot for myself, raised a toast to my uncle, and drank it, and then I poured another for the *Kamis* around me. I shared my drink with the gods so that perhaps they would share some of their wisdom with me.

Funny enough, the more I drank, the easier it was to talk to them.

Kidding. Sort of...

With a completely sober mind, I started speaking to the gods, or kamis, around me. The word 'kami' comes from the Japanese spiritual belief of Shintoism. Essentially, the belief is that all things, such as mountains, rivers, animals, and places, have spiritual energy, or kami. At least, this is just my understanding of it at a surface level. Some of these places have more spiritual energy than others, which allows for a better connection.

I think I have always felt kami around me, especially in nature, since I always feel myself become more grounded. Nature has always soothed my soul—the way a warm breeze feels, the sun on my face, the smells of the different trees, and the songs of birds chirping. All of it is captured inside of me and plays like a gentle song, stilling the stormy seas of my mind. I have always felt most connected with this energy when I hike mountains. I have hiked five at this point, and they were all something remarkable for me. I think I am just captivated by the mesmerizing beauty of the view; it almost feels as close to flying as I could get in this lifetime. I think when I am at the top, there is a sense of clarity I get, and it puts all things in perspective. It makes me feel connected with what I want in life: peace.

Perhaps my desire for peace draws me to war against myself, to break out of this pathetic mindset. Perhaps that is just my nature.

With firm roots, I plant myself into the ground to achieve self-confidence and certainty. I am a rock and metal; I am enduring and stubborn, unmovable with my principles and values. I am malleable and shapeless. I can flow like water, I can press through rock, and I can carve paths through pure persistence. Though the surface tension may break, I always reconstruct myself—differently, perhaps, but whole. I am wind, and I am fire. Each breath stokes the embers of my passion.

Once again, I had closed my eyes, but this time in meditation. I followed my breath and focused on my heartbeat. I began to let go.

I could feel the presence of kami around me—the energy is just in the air, vibrating. I focused on it to match it, feel it, and integrate it into myself.

Locked in, I visualized a flame burning inside of me, a single light in a black void. I inhaled sharply to stoke the flame. My nostrils flared, my diaphragm expanded, and my chest rose as I brought this life energy inside of me. At the end of my inhale, I held the life within me for a moment, then sharply released it again. The flame was calm for a moment, only to burn again with the next life breath. I was combing my knowledge of Wim Hof breathing and Zen meditation to create my own form.

It almost felt like I was calling on my own name, a name that I could not speak in any language, but something far more profound: the name of my truest self, the essence of my very soul.

With each breath, I called him: "Wake up! Move! You are alive! BREATHE!"

The forcefield between my heart and mind was rattling. What was once unshakable and firm seemed brittle and made of glass. I felt my heart beating faster as I warred against the barriers within me that were preventing me from progressing.

Then, it happened: the flame within me raged and exploded inside of its confinement. The forcefield cracked and shattered. I was free again! I burned even greater than before, and the glass melted, burning away into grains of sand.

I opened my eyes for the first time in a while, and I broke through the fog. This endless haze of depression once clouded my judgment. It felt like I was crying from relief, but there were no tears, as they had all evaporated inside me. Instead, I just felt my own energy, revitalized, steaming off of me.

I must maintain balance within myself so that I can breathe freely. Each breath I take is a gift from the kamis of this beautiful world. I am a life that grew from life. The essence of the world is part of me. All living things are tied to life energy whether they realize it or not. I have to stay tapped into this energy, to remain free.

Freedom is the only thing that ever truly mattered to me, and I was in a prison of my own making, crafted by depression. The door was closed but never locked; I was just too defeated to lift myself up, to try again. I felt so lost, having lost my wife and everything else in between. I didn't know what was next for me. I couldn't see a path, or rather I didn't want to acknowledge a path without her. I procrastinated and procrastinated on forming my new plan, and I left room for error in case things changed between us. I put my life on hold, trying to be patient like the mountain, but now it was time for me to let go like the wind.

In my reflection, I gazed at the mountainside and felt the icy cold wind brush against my face. In my mind's eye, I let my heart open again, and when I did, I let the wisp of "her" go. I watched it float away through the valleys, through the trees, and through all their leaves until it was out of my sight.

I spoke softly to myself, but aloud: "I love you so much, I miss you even now, but I am done waiting. I need to pick up the pieces."

Then I said in my head, *"Serendipity! I surrender to you. I am done fighting you. I don't need to know the path anymore! I simply trust that I know absolutely nothing! I accept that life will never happen exactly the way that I plan it to, but as long as I strive forward, I will come closer to my goal. I surrender my whole heart to you. Show me the path! Guide me with compassion and integrity! Surprise me along the way!"*

I laughed to myself in sweet surrender.

I give up!

Then I thought it was an appropriate time to take an oath. I looked for the words and then found them. I smiled to myself as I came to the only logical conclusion. Inspired by my favorite author, Brandon Sanderson, I said:

"Life before death.
Strength before weakness.
Journey before destination."

I've always understood the first two lines but never truly embraced the third. Well, here I am, a changed man.

With another small chuckle about what a nerd I am, I grabbed Miss Tsuki, tucked her into her backpack carrier, and began trekking back down the mountain.

My little fox girl wasn't even completely tired out from the hike, but I decided to give her a little break. Sometimes you just want to carry your children.

As we made our way down, there were new hikers on their way up. I extended my congratulations to them and told them they were near the peak, as the other hikers had done to me.

Tsuki rested quietly in my backpack. She fell fast asleep, and I could feel how calm and relaxed she was. I thanked her for accompanying me all the way to the top. "I'm glad you convinced me to take you along. I hope you feel your persistence was rewarded." I also warned her that there are many more mountains to come and that she should take this opportunity to rest.

I slipped a few times going down the mountain but eventually reached my car. I loaded a sleepy Shiba Inu girl into the front seat, buckled her up, turned on my *Mistborn* audiobook, and hit the road.

Quick tangent:

* To any critical eyes that recognize that title, I am aware that my first quote was from *The Way of Kings* and not *Mistborn*. I'm not lying, I'm a big fan!

Anywho, after a short drive, we made it home, and we feasted on a big brunch! For Tsuki, I made her tuna and eggs, her favorite! I had a burger and a healthy portion of fries, thus making it an unhealthy portion.

After our quick refuel, we ventured outside to the Three Old Goat's Brewery, which happened to be attached to the Airbnb I was staying at. I ordered a flight of different beers to taste, grabbed my laptop and a book, and embraced the serendipity of my day!

Tsuki sat on my lap as I typed away at new stories, ideas, goals, and research. Before I knew it, my beers had run dry, and the sun had set.

As the day drew to a close, I lingered outside, savoring the crisp evening air and the warmth of Tsuki's embrace. In her unwavering loyalty, I found solace and strength, reaffirming my commitment to charting a course guided by love and resilience. Amidst the vast expanse of the night sky, I whispered words of reassurance to my faithful companion, knowing that together we would weather life's storms and embrace the journey, one step at a time.

"Everything is going to be alright, Bub, just me and you. I'm so grateful to have you in my life, and I'm always going to take care of us. Together, we are going to figure this all out."

Chapter 4
FLIGHT OF THE HAWK

November 4, 2022

As my alarm blared, I was met with the jubilant presence of Tsuki. Her energetic wiggle and affectionate gestures welcomed me to a new day. Taking a few extra moments in bed, I relished the simple joy of being with her, mindful of every scratch and cuddle. Ever since losing my beloved mini-schnauzer, Fritz, I've made it a point to savor these moments, capturing them in memory and sometimes in photos.

I reached out, and she buried her head in my hand. With a few neck scratches, she was putty in my hands as she rolled over, a glutton for lovin'.

As 10 minutes stretched into 15 minutes, I rolled out of bed, planted my hands on the cement floor, and paused. I looked at the floor and hesitated in my mind. Part of me was saying, "Do some push-ups." That's what is normally there for me, but an alternative voice just said, "Why bother? Just hurry up and get ready." I leaned into my weaker inclination, using "time management" as my excuse not to act. I crawled to my feet and started gathering my boxes and bags as I prepared for my next trek. I paused for another moment and stared at the boxes, and with a sigh I said, "My time in Virginia had come to an end! Onwards!"

McAffee Knob had some answers for me, and I felt that I was slowly reclaiming my identity. I intended to hike the Tinker trail as well; unfortunately, the weather had other plans for me. My last possible hiking day was rained out. I considered making the hike regardless of the inclement weather but then read that "the wooden steps on the trail are perilous when slippery" and decided to use my better judgment. Sometimes I just want to power through the hardship and the suffering to prove to myself that I can do it, and other times, I fear breaking my leg on the mountain alone. You win some, and you lose some. Maybe one of these days I'll be dramatic enough to do that, but today, I'll choose to be wise.

I began plotting out a different course of action. I wanted to go to the local museum; however, they found my idea of bringing Tsuki along in a backpack to be grotesque and unimaginable. That lead me to ignore the bunch of stuck-up, snooty historians and take a different course of action that would enable me to bring the puppers along. Tsuki and I said, "See you later, losers," and went to Black Dog Salvage, which was a pretty popular thrift/antique shop in the area.

She wiggled her way into the backpack, and we went on our way! Black Dog Salvage was a good first stop. I enjoyed the vibrant community that was there and browsed aimlessly throughout the store in hopes of finding something beautiful. I particularly liked the gallery section upstairs and was captivated by an acrylic painting.

The painting was a large landscape about 6ft in width and 3ft in height. Art is most beautiful when it resonates with the right person. Art is subjective; it isn't so much about being good or bad, but about the feeling it evokes.

This is coming from a person that makes drawing stick figures look difficult. Then again, some lunatics are willing to pay 120k for a banana duct taped to a wall ...

I saw a lush mountain scape, a green boundless valley, and a full blue sky. In the sky, a single hawk was soaring high above the mountains, alone but free. The painting stirred that deep longing in me for freedom. I've always imagined the feeling of flying, the clarity of rising above all my earthly attachments to dare to swim in the infinite sea of the gods. I think in my heart I've always felt weighed down by the pressure I put on myself to succeed. I try to be strong for my family, friends, and myself; however, at times it just feels like I'm lying to myself. I want to be free, but I feel so trapped, and often it feels like the goal is just getting further away from me like a mirage of an oasis in the desert. I'm just dying of thirst trying to carve this opportunity for myself. I keep stretching my hand forward to just touch the cusp of my potential, yet it pulls away from me at the last moment, just beyond my fingertips.

As I gazed at the painting, tears started to well in my eyes. I felt this has been happening to me much more frequently than usual, and the reservoir of tears within me that I held behind concrete dams started breaking through the cracks. Water is life, and it always finds a way through the stone, especially a heart of stone. I smiled to myself as I thought, *"Do you think the hawk thinks he is free? Or do you think he wonders why he can't fly indefinitely without exhaustion settling in?"*

Freedom is a state of mind, and in some ways this world is a matrix, governed by the placebo effect. We are the summation of what we think we are. If we feel trapped, alone, and broken, we are. If we believe we are limitless, lucky, and at peace, we are. Our minds govern our reality, and only we can truly decide what is real and what is fake, what is possible and what is impossible. I have read incredible stories about the placebo effect and how our minds can bend reality around what we think is possible. Some people heal diseases through faith or self-belief, some people can walk when they are told they never would again, and some women bear children when they are told that they are infertile.

Stop listening to other people define your limitations! RAGE! RAGE! Rage against what others try to condition you to believe. Whose will is stronger, yours or theirs? Do not submit; your resolve must be unshakable in this invisible wrestling match of spirit. If you believe you are limited by some "genetic limit" or some wall of challenges ahead of you, you are. Stop telling yourself convenient lies to justify cowardice or laziness. It is your life, be bold.

There have been countless times through human history when ingenuity, tenacity, and boldness defeated the opinions of "experts" and academics who said, "It cannot be done." I honestly believe we as human beings are infinitely more capable than we realize; we barely challenge ourselves to truly reach for our potential. I often think that nothing in the world is done unintentionally, that there is intelligence to everything, and that intelligence is not always compassionate. It feels like we are constantly encouraged to sedate ourselves with frivolity. We overindulge in food, entertainment, and technology. It becomes all-consuming, and it makes it hard to focus and accomplish meaningful work. Separate yourself from everything you are connected to and view yourself as just a human being, all beliefs, likes, and dislikes to the side. Then think to yourself, "What am I leaving on the table? What is the highest incarnation of my potential?" Start seeing through all the distractions and think critically about your life, where it's going, and where you want to be, because if you don't, you will die chained to mediocrity. It is said that before you die, your "life flashes before your eyes."

I think of that moment a lot. I want to leave behind a life I was proud of and make a difference in the world by how I spend my time. Wouldn't it be so sad to find out that you were always capable of more, but you just didn't choose to seize your potential? And for what? Because Tommy in the fourth grade called you fat? Did you get bullied in high school? Have you never felt popular or well-liked? Look for *those feelings* inside of you, those feelings that make you squirm or feel "less than," and face them. True "self-love" is having the courage to face yourself and do the dirty work of sorting through your traumas and limiting beliefs; it is not, saying, "I love myself and I'm perfect." Nobody is perfect. Every single person makes mistakes, and you can either choose to acknowledge your mistakes and bad decisions to grow from them or keep hiding behind convenient lies. You can imitate self-care as part of "personal development" by sharing positive quotes or saying positive things; however, true self-development is messy, grueling work.

Think about how often you sacrifice your long-term goals for short-term pleasures. Think of all the times that you hit the snooze button on your alarm because "you need your rest today." Think about it when you are eating junk food that serves you no real nutritional purpose. Imagine what you could achieve if you dared to ask more of yourself. Imagine the most powerful physical version of yourself: your full genetic potential met, a person fully realized. Imagine what the smartest version of you feels like and how good it feels to be knowledgeable and helpful to those around you. Imagine the most fulfilled version of yourself putting your head down on your pillow at the end of a day of hard work. The biggest mountain that we all face is the mountain of our own bullshit. Just remember this: "Cowards make excuses." I'm so tired of all the "I can't" mentality that is ready to roll off the tips of everyone's tongues. NO, YOU CAN. It's hard, but stop being a coward; hard work sows the seeds of excellence. Till the fields, enrich the soil, and grow! BE FREE, or DIE never truly knowing what you are capable of.

Sorry if that was intense, but that's a lecture I've given myself a million times. Maybe it can help you. I just want you to realize that there is so much in the world that we don't understand yet, but we need to try and bridge that gap to grow. If we don't strive to become better, we just become miserable wretches that bog down on the dreams of others. I'm just always so shocked at how easily people give up, and I know all it is is fear of failure. Don't fear failure or looking like a fool if your heart is in the right place. We aren't always going to come off the way want in the world, but you know what? You aren't under a microscope. Everyone else is similarly distracted with their own mountains of bullshit. Don't be afraid. You only have one shot at this, so don't be a coward that never tries. Don't you dare give up before you even start. Change is possible, and it begins the instant you decide you are ready for it. It doesn't have to wait until Monday, your birthday, or the new year. Time is slipping through your fingers, and you need to get into gear.

I felt inspired by the art, but less inspired by the price tag. I also didn't even have a spot to put it right now because I was traveling. It was weird not having a home base, a hearth fire at the center of my home filling me with warmth. Now I was just the wind, breezing by as I observe all that I see. I was just collecting stories, moments, and instances of inspiration. I laughed to myself, thinking it was ironic that I couldn't afford to buy freedom, but I could afford the time to dream about it. Less dreaming and more action—I need to find equilibrium. My dreams flow like water but must be tangible and strong, like earth.

I continued on my little serendipitous adventure and found myself at an antique shop. To be honest, this was more of what I was looking for, rather than what I found before. I love treasure hunting, looking for those weird and strange things that just spark something within you.

With Tsuki on my back, I explored the store and found things of intrigue and nostalgia. I laughed as I saw that some games I played as a kid were considered antiques, and I felt a pull on my heartstrings when I saw a Hotwheels truck. I was amazed that it was still in its original casing and fiddled with it in my hands as I looked at all angles of it, confirming my suspicion. This was the exact model of Hotwheels that my brother and I had as kids. I remembered this purple truck to be one of his favorites. It's so crazy how far gone the times of us playing with our Hotwheels are, and us just violently crashing them into each other. I decided that it had found its home and that I had to bring it back with me. Funny enough, I had recently bought another Hotwheels from childhood, a yellow Lamborghini Murcielago, that was my favorite as a kid. It was like a funny reunion—they found their way back to us after all these years.

I continued to explore the store and came across some interesting rings. The collector explained to me that the ring was a Navajo storyteller ring. Apparently each is supposed to be unique and has interesting designs carved into it. Fully understanding that she totally could have been lying to me, I still bought it. It was a nice ring that depicted an eagle in flight. It felt aligned for me to purchase it, an eagle in flight, freedom resting on my hand. Perhaps this ring belonged to another dreamer like me, and now the weight of those dreams fell into my hands, too. I cannot afford to fail for both myself and my predecessor.

Shortly after my purchase, I retired back to my Air Bnb with Miss Tsuki, had a nice lunch, and got right back to work.

I'm grateful for the time I spent in VA, but now I am off to my next destination, Maryland—or as I used to say as a college student, "Fucking Maryland." That is honestly only funny to me and like three other people, but basically, I had gone once before with some friends, and everything kept going wrong. We were freezing to death camping at some lame EDM rave. The entire trip was a disaster, but I digress.

This stay ended up being one of my favorites because it was homey, and driving through the town made me feel like I was in one of my Papa's snowy wintery towns he would build at Christmas time with all his ornaments. The town was filled with curves and hills that gave it a vaguely globelike appearance that was familiar and nostalgic. My grandfather passed away a few years ago, and it gave me a warm and sentimental feeling to remember him like that. I miss our long conversations on the phone and his rancorous, infectious laughter. We had many good times just joking about anything, and I'd always try my hardest to make him laugh because his laugh genuinely brought me joy.

The house I stayed at was historic, but I'm not going to lie, it was a little spooky. My heart dropped when my door opened in the middle of the night, but I realized my alleged paranormal activity was more of an issue with the door latch not having a deadbolt hole to rest in. Therefore, in the middle of the night, it opened without so much as a breeze and terrified me. This haunt was a simple fix of barricading my door shut at night so I didn't have to live with the terror. Although that solved one problem, it did not solve the ghostly apparition lurking in the corner of my room.

Kidding.

After a few days of getting used to the haunts of this old house, it felt like home for a bit. Tsuki was the most relaxed she had been, and even I was quite pleased with the ways that things were flowing at work. One of my coworkers came back from paternity leave, and I was so grateful that I could finally breathe again by giving back his work. For the first time in three months, my job wasn't burning me out. I had time in my mornings to work on my myriad personal projects such as writing this book, writing two other books, trading, and photography. I was finally feeling some peace after months of turbulence and destruction. I even treated myself to a nice bottle of Dewar's Scotch to celebrate this newfound shift in the tides of war. My enemy was finally done punching and ultimately punched themselves out tired. Now it was time for REVENGE!

I started using a trick I hadn't employed in a while, which is inadvertently thanks to my "brother" Lag. We are similar people, and when we get passionate about something it is just "pedal to the metal," fury, and a hellbent desire to succeed. He kept dropping motivational YouTube videos into our group chat, and it led me down an old rabbit hole. Back in the days when I would train at 4 a.m. I would use motivational speeches as my alarm to get me out of bed when I hesitated.

I was working out with my X3 Bar, calisthenics, and shadowboxing. There happened to be a mirror in the living room, and I was looking into it as I was working out, trying to catch a glimpse into my future self, the man that I was creating.

This Youtube video was titled "Be Ruthless" by Motiversity, and from 6:27–9:33 in that video, there was a direct message to me:

"In this very moment, all you have is all you need.

What would you like to do,
what do you believe you were destined to do?
...

You have a date with destiny, you have
unfinished business, and it is time for you to go back
to the drawing board with a new perspective
...

Perspective is what changes the game! Stop complaining about the divorce! Stop complaining about the job loss.
Are you going to complain in the face of conflict?!
Or are you going to seize the opportunity?!

What if losing the job was the opportunity?!
What if the divorce was the opportunity?!

I'm talking to that person that grew up without a father!
I'm talking to that person that is acquainted with pain!
I'm talking to that person that knows what it's like to come from NOTHING! So you literally have nothing to lose!
The only thing that is in your hand, IS A DREAM!
The only thing that is in your hand is, "I HAVE WHAT IT TAKES TO GET TO THE TOP OF THAT HILL!

Will you buckle under the pressure?!
OR WILL YOU RISE TO THE OCCASION?!

You are not dead yet! You may be tired, but you are not dead! You have the opportunity to rise above what happened to you! You have to make it up in your mind that all you have, is all you need!

I know it hasn't been easy
...
it's time to win
The only person that is going to help you,
is that person in the mirror.
This is the hardest grind you are ever
going to have to do in your life.
You are powerful.
You are relentless.
You are enough.
You just got to step into your fucking power."

I tell you what ...that woke me up! I was so tired. I had been struggling for so long. With the echoes of the motivational words reverberating in my mind, I embarked on a rigorous workout, channeling my inner strength and determination. With each rep and each breath, I reaffirmed my commitment to greatness, refusing to be bound by the limitations of the past. I looked at myself in the mirror, and I took it personally. I felt the fire come back to me behind my eyes and in my heart. I was done holding out for my ex-wife. I was done hoping that she would come back and that things could make sense. It was time to get the fuck on and do so with an ungodly intensity. I just looked in the mirror and boxed. I was killing that man, killing the old me. He needed to die, I was done making excuses. I was just so done with feeling broken. It just didn't matter anymore. Nothing from the past mattered anymore. It was time to seize the opportunity!

I dropped into my X3 sets and watched my muscles contract with each rep, absolute control, absolute intention. I worked until complete failure in each movement. Then I dropped into calisthenics, combining Wim Hof breathing for recovery and diaphragmatic breathing to oxygenate my blood so I could increase my overall output. I started working on my handstand pushups, leaning against the wall for balance. I just let out all of the frustration I was holding onto. Just pure effort, I let myself get loud and grunt and yell through all of it. I just completely let go of all my self-restraint. I needed to bring out an animal, a demon, a savage mindset.

There was just one word in my head, "More!" Enough was enough, and I needed to free myself from the binds of this depression. This noose collars me to mediocrity. No, no one has this power over me. No one can steal my fire. I am fire, it is my nature. BREATHE! Each breath is freedom! It is autonomy! Give yourself purpose!

After about two hours, I can honestly say that every muscle in my body had worked until failure. I just laid back on the carpeted floor, closed my eyes, and told myself, "This is you, don't fucking lose him again." Tsuki then came up to me and started giving me some kisses as I laid back, and I knew that "right here, right now, I have everything that I need."

My laptop was in the other room. It was the key to my financial freedom. My X3 lay at my feet, an enemy vanquished, and my dog at my side, true loyalty, honor, and integrity. I had everything I needed. I have always had everything I need, and I can and will do more. I had to protect this headspace. I had to advance.

Many people may try to deceive you in life, to convince you that you are less than you are. However, you must not try to deceive yourself. Do not tell yourself you are incapable, less than, or unworthy, because you will believe it. The simplest and hardest thing to do is to flip the script. Whenever you find yourself saying you can't make a positive change that would benefit your life, do it anyway. Stop telling yourself that you are limited by the circumstances of your birth and upbringing and become an outlier in your environment. You must become unreasonable; limitations can only be decided by you, and even when you think you have found them, you are always welcome to challenge them again if you change your mind.

Life is happening right now, so do not lose yourself in the troubles of your past or in your anxieties of the future. Fight for today.

As I lay spent on the floor, bathed in the glow of accomplishment and the warmth of Tsuki's affection, I realized that true freedom lies not in the absence of obstacles, but in the relentless pursuit of excellence. With renewed vigor and unwavering resolve, I embraced the challenges ahead, ready to seize the opportunity and carve my own path in the world.

In the quiet of the night, with the stars as my witness, I vowed to never again falter in the face of adversity. For I am the architect of my fate, the master of my destiny, and with each passing moment, I am one step closer to greatness.

Chapter 5

FROSTBITTEN DREAMS AND FIRELIT HORIZONS

December 17, 2022

After my time in Maryland came to an end, I made my trek back to my hometown for the holidays in November. To be honest, I wasn't particularly excited to be going there, but I felt guilty about trying to travel to Europe after Maryland because I had the chance to be "home for the holidays." I knew it would not be taken well if I didn't return, but part of me just wanted to be alone for a while. I was worried about old dynamics arising and being pulled into a role I left behind. I just didn't want to be in the dynamic of being in the same house as my mother and my brother. I just wanted peace and quiet.

My drive took about five hours, so I just relished in the freedom and the views along the way. I tried to be more optimistic about returning home and told myself I would be happy to see "the boys" and some of my other home friends. It had been about three years since I saw most of them, but maybe this was what I needed. Maybe friends and family would ultimately lift my spirits and further push me to where I was striving to be.

Tsuki slept for most of the ride, and I called friends to pass the time as we made plans to meet. I also enjoyed listening to the seventh book in Brandon Sanderson's *Mistborn* series—things were spicing up in there! I just love this man's mind and creativity, it's 10/10 recommendation every single time. I just pray that Amazon Prime never gets the rights to make any movies for him, because season one of *The Wheel of Time* was an utter disappointment to people who read the books. There is no greater arrogance than a TV show changing the facts of the core doctrine and spirit of an amazing best-selling book. Don't even get me started on *Dragon Ball: Evolution* or the live-action *Avatar: The Last Air Bender*. STICK TO THE SOURCE MATERIAL! TRUST THE SOURCE MATERIAL! It was tested and successful.

Please keep your own "vision" out of the waters of the author's masterpiece! However, I digress, and I am heavily biased, yet I still hate lazy storytelling and betraying the ethos set by the author. One more complaint before I get back on track: *Game of Thrones*, season 7. "What were you thinking?!" Clearly, either the Night King's dragon or Drogon should have blown fire on Jon Snow. This in turn would have revealed that he is a Targaryen and perhaps "awakened" his latent Targaryen traits. After the fire fails to burn him, it would reveal him as the true heir to the Iron Throne. However, instead, they decided to make just one of the most anti-climatic and disappointing endings to a great show.

Okay, I'm done now...

I was "steel-pushed" out of the world of *Mistborn* and into the world of Mastic, NY. As I took Exit 58 off of Sunrise Highway, my heart began to race as I saw the familiar sights of the town I felt I had escaped many years ago. Honestly, I have a fair amount of disdain for this town because it just reminds me of times in my life that were particularly difficult. Yet I was called back home to face these old demons and put them to rest. I needed to reconcile this part of my life. I left, but when I did, I suppose things were unresolved and needed to be squared off in a karmic sort of way.

I counted to myself silently—*one, two, three, four, five, six, seven*—as I passed the various homes I have lived in this area growing up. Each one of these places held energy from a time in my life. I thought about who I was in each one of those arcs, how I had changed, the mistakes I made, and things I wish I knew. I thought about old friends, girlfriends, and just the weird times of high school. 2023 was just around the corner, and I was thinking to myself, "Wow, has it really been 10 years since I graduated high school?" Yet it still seems so fresh in my memory. The next decade of my life lurks in the shadowy path ahead, but in my heart, I'm still 21. I'm sure a lot of people can relate to that feeling. Where does time go? In just a few more years, it'll have been 10 years since I graduated college. That will be a sobering day, which will then be remedied with a healthy pour of whiskey.

---

*Steel pushing is a power utilized by allomancers. Allomancers are known as Mistings and Mistborn, *for the most part*. They consume specific metals and then "burn" the metals inside of them to activate their allomantic powers. In this case, steel pushing would be utilized by a Steel Misting or Mistborn and enables the user to push other metals away from them. If done precisely, it can simulate flying.

Around the time I finished college, I watched the finale of *The Office*, and one of the characters said, "I wish I knew we were living in the good ol' days when we were living them." I often think about this line as I accept and observe that the days of my life count down to an inevitable demise. I'm 27 now, and things haven't gone quite as I expected. The thought of getting married again crossed my mind, as did having kids ...a little bit of dread poured in as I thought to myself, *how could I possibly love someone enough, soon enough, to get married and have kids with them?* With a large sigh, I allowed that thought to slip away, as it was not important to deal with right now.

I passed my old high school as I approached my destination. It was funny how it was bigger than my college. It stood there eerily in the night, soaked in the memories of a time in my life I truly hated. I didn't hate high school so much in the angsty teenager way, but more in the "I cannot fathom the violence, stupidity, and mediocrity of this prison" kind of way. I strived for success, drowning myself in AP classes so that one day I could put as much distance as possible between me and high school after graduation. Fights were commonplace in this school to the point where it was a valid reason to be late to class. It was so frequent that most students who passed their freshman year were desensitized to the violence and just found it to be a hindrance.

Every day I was on guard. I tried not to make enemies, especially with those deemed both violent and stupid, because that cocktail appeared to be detrimental to my academic success and to my overall escape. I laughed to myself, as one thought crossed my mind: "Fuck high school." My millennial self felt some sort of release from that, and I imagined many others must feel the same way. Sometimes you just have to let shit go.

Whatever, high school was 10 years ago. It was the crucible that helped shape you into the person you are today. We have to pay homage to our past, but we must also let the weight of it go. I suppose I have been carrying some pieces of it with me still. Although I hated my time there, I grew from it, and there were some good moments. Everything is just a learning process. Those kids weren't violent or stupid; they just learned those behaviors from bad parents and systems that didn't catch them when no one else did. What I really see when I look back is a bunch of kids that were given up on. They leaned into bad habits learned in their environment and acted out in school. For some, it was probably a cry for help, and for others, maybe it was a way to feel powerful when they felt powerless at home. I just wish we were all given a fair chance out of the gate of life, but we just aren't. We are all different and have experienced different comforts afforded to us. What some of us take for granted, like having parents that love us, heat and electricity in the house, or food in the fridge, others are in want of.

I was going through my own struggle in high school and was blind to the possibility that others may be struggling, too. Maybe I wasn't completely blind to it, but I certainly see much more than I once did. I have learned to take perspective from that time and to have some gratitude and compassion for myself and others that shared in that experience.

Life isn't inherently fair, but it is up to you to balance the scale. If you need to have a chip on your shoulder, then so be it. If you feel that you desire more than you have, do the work. No one is entitled to an easy life, but some are gifted with it. Ironically, those who are gifted with a life of leisure tend to self-destruct emotionally because they have not endured the feelings of "want." Every single person you see struggles with something, just not necessarily in the same way you would struggle with something.

With that in mind, I balanced the books of high school in my head and decided to "let sleeping dogs lie." This part of my life was over, just as another part of my life was now over. It was time to move on and look ahead. Don't be afraid of what you once were; you have grown beyond that person with each day that passes.

We have the amazing ability to pivot on a dime and completely change the person we are at any given moment. If you don't feel that way, it is because your mind is shackled by fear: fear of failure, fear of judgment, fear of the work, fear of the sacrifice, and unwillingness to try to change. Going forward, when you tell yourself or proclaim to someone else that you "cannot do something," I need you to ask yourself why you feel so limited. Entertain a hypothetical world where that arduous task is possible, and explore how it would be done. Don't think about you doing the work, think only of the task and how it would be completed. IF! You can conclude that some person out there, someway, somehow, can complete the task, then ask yourself, "Why can't I do it, too?"

Perhaps one of my favorite TV shows is *Peaky Blinders*, and the character I resonate the most with is Thomas Shelby. He frequently has others criticize his actions or try to define his limitations. They will tell him in moments of loss, "This is your fault because you consistently fail to acknowledge your limitations!" Yet even when steeping in the bitter brew of failure, or defeat, he will say, "I have no limitations." That sentence is the definition of resolve; that is the mindset you need to embrace when facing problems. You are many things, but you are certainly not powerless to change the trajectory of your life—especially when you fail in a spectacular way, people will tell you why they were right and you were wrong. They pretend to clean the wounds of your defeat but just rub salt in with their cynicism.

Even when you fail, you must reassess and adapt to overcome all obstacles. You don't have to tackle all of your problems in one day, but you can start chipping down on them. If you wait for optimal circumstances, you will never begin. You need to take dramatic action and be prepared to endure suffering to get ahead. The task may be arduous and intimidating, but it is possible! Just always remember that when you are at the point where you are ready to give up, "it is possible." Feed that possibility with your attention and devotion to its growth, and one day you will reap its fruits.

Have you heard of the expression "crabs in a bucket"? If a crab is caught in a trap with other crabs, the other crabs will not allow him to escape despite the door being open. They will rip him apart and pull him back in. Ambition is like that: most people don't have the guts to dare and rebel beyond their limitations. As a result, they need to justify their complacency by dragging you down to their level. People often will tell you that they want to see you do well; however, they rarely want to see you do better than them.

In your heart, mind, and spirit, you must resolve yourself to be limitless. A leader must see the vision when others do not. Hold yourself to a higher standard, even if everyone tells you you are crazy. Create a standard of excellence, even if you have no one in your immediate life to show you the path. We cannot wait to be saved by someone else, and we cannot resign ourselves to perceived limitations. You must rise to become a leader, because the fact that you didn't have anyone to turn to clearly shows that there is a position to fill in your community. You need to rise to the occasion, fill the void, correct the wrongs you see, and show others a better path. The circumstances of our birth and upbringing are all dumb luck. Maybe we hit the lottery and get everything we need, but most people don't; we all feel like we are missing a piece in some shape or form. You can choose to accept that you are lacking the thing that would make you feel whole, or you can seek it out.

If there are no leaders in your family, friends, or community to turn to, then buy a book, listen to a podcast, or watch an interview about someone you think is inspiring. Stop making excuses, and stop blaming your upbringing, your environment, or your "luck" for the lack of results you want to create in your life. Wake up, seek knowledge, and act.

You have no limitations except the ones you accept. Our bodies will respond to the standards our minds enforce. I often convey that feeling to myself by saying, "don't live as a coward." Cowards make excuses for their inability to overcome hardships. There is nothing special about your hardship, and there is no free pass on life because you think you had a rough go of it. Escape your whiney victim mentality and seize the opportunities presented to you. If you can't see the opportunity, carve it out of the earth with your fingernails. Be prepared to suffer, embrace it, and overcome it. *Life is suffering,* but how long you suffer is entirely up to you. Drink in the sweet nectar of hardship and let it fuel you to persevere despite it all. You owe it to yourself to rebel and demand more of yourself. We are a blank canvas of unlocked potential. I promise you, you have no idea who you are or what you are capable of if you have never tried to be more.

My train of thought broke slightly as I saw one last thing before turning into the community where my mother and brother lived. I saw "TJ's Heros," an iconic location in our town. They had some of the best hot sandwiches you can get anywhere, and there were many times when I stayed late at school for extracurricular activities, like debate or sports, and those sandwiches fueled me! It was nostalgic to see it not just still standing, but actually better than before. They used to have a much smaller location, but the years were favorable to them, and they now have a huge location just down the road from their old one.

When I looked at it, I thought, "It doesn't take much. Just keep showing up. Success doesn't have to be some grand thing—it could be as simple as selling sandwiches. Just find something, do it well, and serve your community."

I pulled into the entrance, and my mom rushed over to get the gate for me. I could tell she was ecstatic to see me and to have her "boys" home. I got out of the car, and she gave me a mom-sized hug, and it was nice. It struck me that I hadn't hugged anyone in a couple of months. Well, not *anyone*, but just not as much as I once had. Something that was a normal part of my day had now become such a rarity. How bizarre.

My mom couldn't contain her excitement, but unfortunately, I could not meet her there. I was even a little vexed. I was happy to see them both, but at the same time, the circumstances of my return were not jovial in nature. It was hard to see her so excited when I was just barely digging myself out of the rut. It made me realize that they wouldn't be able to read the room with how I was feeling, so I had to explain in clear terms where I was at. However, I was delighted that my mom made my childhood favorite, lamb stew.

My friends make fun of the way I say "stew" because apparently, I say it the British way because of my mother's accent and it not being a word I frequently use. I understood she was just trying to soothe my broken heart a little, but unfortunately, that is the one wound a parent cannot fix. Despite already knowing that they will try in futility, it is an honorable thing, but perilous nonetheless. Any sort of overtly mom-like behavior was going to annoy me, but I appreciated the subtle things she did to help me be more comfortable.

Whenever I get upset with my mom, I'm plagued with the guilt of the knowledge that she is going to die someday, and I'm going to miss her. That usually brings me to curb my emotions when they are sharpest, but this time around, I needed to be direct and set healthy boundaries for myself emotionally. This can be achieved through love, patience, and honesty. When I caught myself getting frustrated, as we all do with our parents, I just slowed down and made myself calm. Just because you feel an emotion come to the surface doesn't mean you have to react to it. You should pause at times to observe your emotions while you are experiencing them and try to understand why you are feeling them.

I realized the reason why I was getting upset was that I didn't want to feel powerless or broken. I had just found strength in myself again, and I didn't want to feel coddled or to be looked at as a wounded animal.

My family is a rather emotional bunch, and I tend to be a bit of a peacemaker. I don't like to see conflict around me because it disturbs my sanguinity and saps my emotional stamina.

Being "home" made me reflect on the way I would deal with conflict as a kid. I hate hearing yelling, loud arguments, or disrespectful things being said around me. It sets me on edge like how it did when I would hear my parents argue. I just never understood why people couldn't talk calmly to each other. Even when I'm angry, I reel my emotions in so that I don't hurt other people. I know what it's like to have venom seep from my fangs, but I'm unwilling to bite because I know how much it will hurt the other person. I was generally pretty careful with my words, but there were some hard pills I had to swallow about how I tend to emotionally pacify others when they are reactive because I'm trying to stop things from escalating. I realized I needed to change the way I handled conflict and be more direct about my needs as well. I always felt weird asking for my needs to be met because this never felt important to others, or if I said I needed something, I would have to debate for its approval. I also tried to not put my emotions on others because I felt that they didn't care or that my emotions were a burden to them.

I would always remark to my brother, Matthew, that I admired his brazen attitude and how he could say whatever he wanted despite how it could affect other people. My brother explained that if he was upset, someone was going to know about it. That was a thought that felt foreign to me. I'm not a particularly emotionally reactive person, so I can always keep it on a leash while the other person doesn't. I have always thought of it as a blatant "weakness" if you cannot control your emotions or your emotional reactions. However, I realized that I may have overcorrected and not expressed myself enough. My brother has matured quite a bit, and it was funny to see this hulking man and his full-grown beard in his diesel mechanic uniform. I laughed as my younger brother shared his piece of wisdom with me, it felt funny to have my "little" brother teach me a lesson.

I decided that I needed to be more direct with people and be willing to feel uncomfortable if something needed to be said. I think especially when I predict that the other person will react emotionally and negatively upon me telling them the truth, I hesitate to tell them. However! THE TRUTH SHALL SET YOU FREE!

After catching up with family a little and explaining that I needed some personal space to just cope with this, we came to a better understanding and had a pleasant time being with one another for the holidays. It was nice to have some of mom's cooking and feel some of those old feelings again. My brother would ask me to watch TV with him all the time, and it was funny to me. It made me think of us being kids and how we would always sprawl out on the couch and watch TV. If you grew up with a sibling, you know what I mean. It was just so nostalgic watching a show together, and even more so him asking me to watch it with him. The feeling was sweet, but in my heart, I knew I barely watched TV these days, and I just didn't want to lose grip of the mindset I'd been forming.

I had only just touched my resolve recently in Maryland, and I was afraid of slipping back into a depressive state. I needed to keep progressing forward to preserve myself.

The glass barrier that once acted as a barrier to my inner fire, my resolve to succeed, now lay at my feet as sand. The sand was rich in iron from drinking the blood and sweat I had poured into my dreams. I crouched down and harvested each grain as I pulled them back within me to reform in the burning forge in my soul. I smelt the sand within me, reincorporating my resolve and refining it. The injection of my spirit into the sand acted like carbon binding to the iron to form something new: steel. If I do not fuse my spirit with this steel, it will be too brittle from lack of carbon content. I need to be intentional and understand why I'm doing all of this! All of this endurance, alchemization, and tenacity have a purpose.

My purpose is to serve my community by constantly pushing beyond the barrier that holds us all back, to live without limitation!! I reached within myself and drew a blade from the forge. It was sharp, and the metal was hard but unrefined, still full of impurities. Now I needed to pick up the hammer and STRIKE! I must hammer the metal, I must free the mettle of my mind from impurities. Every investment of my time in myself is to refine the blade. I have to compound these experiences within me, folding the metal over and over. With meticulous intention, passion, and diligence, I would craft a blade that could carve the man I wished to be out of the marble of my potential. It would also slash down any opposition in my path or my past. I must cut ties to the things that no longer serve my mission or best interests. This sense of grief inside of me betrayed my heart, and it betrayed the core tenets of the man I wished to be. I cannot stew in inaction, in complacency, I must progress.

A friend of mine frequently references a quote from my last book to me: "Embrace a mindset that empowers you when you feel defeated." He says that it gives him chills when he thinks about it, and I have to remember that those are my own words. I must practice those ideals or risk being a hypocrite. I have to seek challenges, to grow beyond previous limitations.

I realized that I was ready for another hike, another mountain to climb. I planned on a day to go, and I invited a couple of friends to attend as well if it worked for them—if not, I'd go alone. I have always wanted to hike Bear Mountain, but I never got around to it when I lived in New York. Two of my friends, Justin and Richie, answered the call to adventure, as well as Miss Tsuki. I woke up at 5 a.m. on the day of our hike and was met by my Mom at the door. She said, "It's going to snow today, are you sure you want to go?" I paused and felt instant rebellion inside of me: "Conditions are never perfect, we will make due. If it becomes unsafe, we will make the smartest decision." I didn't have room in my heart for fear anymore. I couldn't let little inconveniences get in the way of the goals I had. I saw that the snow was forecasted in the evening, so there appeared to be a window of time where we could succeed; however, hesitation would result in failure.

I assured my mother, and myself, that "all is well," and that I will make adjustments to my plans according to the weather conditions and succeed despite the potential hazards. I loaded Tsukli into the car and went to go pick up Justin, AKA "Jay." It was good to see my old friend. He was the best man at my wedding, so it was a bit painful to face him after my marriage failed. Nevertheless, I shared my heart with my friend, and he shared his support and encouragement. We've had the fortune of knowing each other since we were five years old and have two decades of friendship and brotherhood underneath our belt. I've always trusted Justin as an advisor and as someone who is highly gifted and capable of "imagining the possibilities" with me. It was nice to be able to see these close friends of mine, because their compassion helped stitch together my sense of identity again. These are people that knew me before *her*, and just by talking with them, I started to rediscover who I was and embrace him into myself again.

Along the way, we met up with my friend Richie, and he treated us to a "New York Standard" breakfast: bacon, egg, and cheese on a roll with salt, pepper, and ketchup. I also had some coffee earlier, so the base needs of the food pyramid were met before we set out on our adventure. We caught up and talked about life, politics, and just little things to pass the time on the way to the mountain. As we approached our destination, it started to flurry, and I grew slightly concerned because it was snowing ahead of schedule. I realized that the altitude may be contributing to the circumstances, but we ultimately determined that we would proceed and adjust as necessary. I laughed because I realized that we were all INTJ-A personality types and that we expediently addressed risks, assessed challenges, and came to a decision. It was nice to be speaking the same language as the people around me and to be able to take decisive action.

We parked the car, and I unloaded my camera and put Tsuki in her little green fox sweater. Then we began trekking up the mountain; the path was steep, and the snow foreshadowed a future challenge, but it all appeared to be doable. About 10 minutes into the trail, though, Justin twisted his ankle. Since he was not keen on the idea of being carried up the mountain, he decided to go wait in the lodge—or perhaps it was all a ruse to get out of hiking in the elements. Justin is always playing chess when everyone else is playing checkers. We were down a man, but we continued to climb the mountain with greater attention to the detail of our footing!

Tsuki only had a one-speed setting as per usual and sprinted her little marshmallow butt up the mountain until she couldn't any longer. As we reached the first outlook, Richie marveled at the beauty below. We only hiked for about an hour at that point and were already being rewarded for our efforts. It made me happy to share this experience with him and introduce him to the true majesty of the outdoors. I knew my friend would appreciate it because he is a philosophical soul, and people who think in broad terms like that are often enamored with the beauty of nature.

As we approached the second outlook, Tsuki pulled out her signature move of standing completely still and refusing to budge another step to indicate that she was done. I rolled my eyes at this little princess and packed her up into the carrier so I could haul her up the mountain. The intensity of the snow increased as we ascended the mountain, and conditions grew colder. I decided to wrap Tsuki up in my scarf to keep her a little extra insulated as we persevered through the inclement weather.

I'm afraid I don't have the words to describe the beauty and serenity of hiking the mountain while it snowed. The snow gently fell from above, and it painted the world around us white and pure. I tried to capture that beauty through the lens of my camera. There were instances of peace as the world seemingly slowed and the leaves on the surrounding foliage reached out to catch flurries like a child sticking out his tongue. We were also surprised to see a small waterfall along the way and were deeply appreciative of the stairs that were carved into the stone of the mountain. I loved the feeling of the cold winter air coursing through me with each inhale. It was nice to experience winter again after a year of being in Florida. I don't think Tsuki resonated with this sense of nostalgia; nevertheless, I was taken, enchanted, by the magic of the moment.

I was glad that I could share the magic of it all with Richie, as nothing makes me happier than seeing people enjoy themselves. The snow offered a rare beauty and implied the challenge for us to overcome it. Richie has a similar mind to me; he is someone who has faced evil in his life but remains a kind soul despite it all. He also has the desire to overcome past limitations and test his mettle. The snow inhibited our path, but we slowed down, paid attention to our footing, and adroitly navigated through the treacherous terrain.

After a short while, we embraced the crowning jewel of our adventure: the peak. The snow engulfed the landscape below and ate the visibility into the distance. We were still able to appreciate the stunning view of the snow-shrouded valley and enjoy an eagle's eye view of the grassy plains and small streams below.

I took Tsuki out of her carrier so she could share at this moment as well. She was sound asleep, happy to be carried by her dad. Her sleepy little eyes peeled open, and her body wiggled with excitement as she climbed out. The snow really started to come down at the peak, and the wind began to increase in intensity as well. I gave my little doge a snuggle and kiss, but before putting her back in the carrier, I wrapped her in my jacket to ensure that she was warm and safe. I grew concerned over the change in temperature and realized that her sweater and my scarf may not be enough to keep her warm. I realized that I knew how to navigate the cold through breathwork, so I assessed the situation and resolved to endure for her sake.

Fortunately, I'm well acquainted with the cold from studying Wim Hof, the "Ice Man." Wim developed his breathing technique as a way to move past the grief of losing his wife to suicide. He often says that cold saved his life and speaks of how it can save the lives of millions more. The cold initiates a stress response in your body, and if you can control that stress response, you can apply that skill to your emotional fortitude as well. Endurance builds a stronger mind and body. Your body will adapt to any means imposed upon it if you consistently try to break through the barrier of normalcy.

At this point, meditation has become a little more mainstream, but to those out there that don't practice it all, Wim's technique is an active form of meditation. You are actively trying to seize control of your mind while enduring an uncomfortable situation, whereas regular meditation is usually done in a calm and safe environment. Although there are many schools of thought on mediation and different ways to approach it, at the core of it all is focusing on your breath, raising your sense of awareness, and reaching for the "void" of nothingness. When you can quiet your mind, you can also quiet all the lurking problems on the back burner. The boiling pot slows to a simmer, and then, stillness. When you reach this brain state, you aren't thinking about anxiety, depression, how burnt out you are, your job, or the bills you have to pay. When you focus on your breath, you are able to synchronize your heart, mind, and spirit into one person: a human being, you. We have to make time to remember that despite wherever we spend 40–80 hours per week as an employee, we are not just worker drones; we are human. Feed your humanity in a world that starves you of it with constant distractions.

My friends have come to expect the unusual from me, so seeing me do this was probably nothing new to them. Richie had seen me do this before when we all went swimming in a waterfall together with some of our friends. The water was frigid, and everyone was hilariously suffering, but with Wim, I was able to swim in the waterfall for about 30 minutes in freezing temperatures. However, this is nothing compared to the incredible feats Wim has accomplished. To put it into perspective, he hiked Mount Everest in shorts and without a shirt, ran a polar marathon, and has several world records for swimming under frozen lakes. Wim has baffled scientists throughout the world by accomplishing the impossible through sheer force of will, and also peace of mind. There have also been some fascinating documentaries of him fighting off diseases when injected with them, maintaining his core body temperature when submerged in ice water, and even just his flexibility. In one interview he was asked how he did it all, and he said with a sharp intensity, "I can do it all, because compared to the pain of grieving heart, it is nothing." That's something I understand now.

I walked away from Richie and asked him for a moment as I began doing some breathwork to get my blood pumping. I focused for about 10 minutes in order to just drink in the cold, but also to stoke the fire within me. With my eyes closed, I could feel the warmth in the center of my chest, and I imagined what it would look like to see my oxygenated blood flow through my body with each breath. After a short while, I was mentally prepared to endure and physically charged to succeed.

I walked a short while in my t-shirt until Richie offered me some reprieve, as he was wearing two layers of jackets and decided to give me one. Part of me didn't want to accept it because it meant that he would also be uncomfortable in the cold as well. I didn't want to inconvenience him over my decision to put my dog's safety first, yet in Richie, I have a true brother. He told me, "Bro, I'm not going to let you suffer in just a t-shirt when I have two layers. I can endure a little cold, too." I hesitated to accept the help but remembered that "The Crew" had proved themselves to me in these last few months. It's okay to accept help sometimes—you don't always have to do it on your own. I've always just struggled to believe that some people just genuinely care and want to help you. I always believed they existed as a concept, but I never felt that they existed in my life. I always needed to be strength incarnate to move forward. I'm self-reliant, but to a fault perhaps.

I accepted the coat and took note of my gratitude for having a friend who would endure challenges with me and look out for me altruistically.

We continued to explore the various paths along Bear Mountain and laughed wholeheartedly as we saw the impending doom on other mountaintops as snow squalls approached in the distance. It was particularly hilarious because we started to recognize the pattern of when the snow would pick up in intensity. We would be swarmed and stormed by the snow in intense intervals but laughed at the suffering together. We got vaguely lost, which tends to happen, but then, in our strategist fashion, we analyzed our position, retraced our steps, and followed a course of action suitable to our escape from the snowy mountain. We walked slowly down the slippery steps at an angle to brace ourselves in case we fell. I always shifted my weight in the direction of the terrain to avoid getting hurt too badly if I lost my footing. While ascending, I always lean forward, and on the descent, I lean backward. It was exhausting maintaining my balance with Tsuki on my back while trying not to slip on the rocks, but after some dedicated effort, we reached the bottom again.

I loved hiking mountains for the view at the top but always wished I could simply fly back down after seeing it; however, that is not the world we live in. The snow was quite heavy at this point, and the small flurries of the morning evolved into thick dollops of ice. We made our way back to the parking lot and checked in on Justin. Jay walked over, his limp miraculously cured from earlier, and we went to get a well-deserved hot meal! Jay has always liked my photography, so I let him live vicariously through the photos I captured along the way, but next time, I'll be sure to get him to the top with better weather conditions. No man shall be left behind, but it was probably for the best that he sat back, since the footing was treacherous along the way. In the words of Brandon Sanderson, he would have been able to move "maladroitly."

We drove to a local coffee shop, and I enjoyed the bliss of the black gold kissing my lips and warming my spirit. It was honestly such a charming venue, and it seemed loved by the locals. There was a lot of warmth in the place, and we sat for a moment, enjoying the live music and holiday cheer. Christmas was around the corner, and that holiday magic was in the air.

Part of me felt sad when I heard certain songs play because it made me realize that this year, I wouldn't have her to celebrate with. This was always my favorite time of year because the world always seemed a little kinder to me. I laughed to myself as I thought of our last Christmas together, and the ones before that. I let myself smile at the thought of the good memories and assured myself that there are even better things to come. The heartache of my realization echoed in the void, but I closed my eyes and swallowed it back down with an intentional deep breath.

Be prepared to endure, seek new heights, and grow from this experience. She was my first true love, but certainly not my last. I have to keep pushing forward for the vision of the beautiful family I will have in the future. I'll have a wife that looks at me with love, children eager to see what Santa brought, and simple traditions of Cinnabons on Christmas and pepper pot. I feel a sense of peace as I soak in the joy of the moment. This Christmas will be quiet compared to that vision, but one day, it can be a reality. This is the time to go inward, a reset on life. How rare it is for life to give you a second chance; it would be best to not squander this opportunity.

It would be best to push harder than ever before and learn about the man that I am growing to be. I have to think about these experiences so that one day, I can share them with my children, so I can encourage them to grow, to endure, and to think deeply about things.

Compared to the pain of a grieving heart, all of this is nothing. The pain is there, but I chip away at it a little each day, and I seize control of the one thing that matters: my mind. Face the pain, endure the pain, and overcome it. Integrate it with your desire to succeed. When our past is dark and our future is uncertain, we must turn to the present moment. Live intentionally and intentionally shape the future through force of will. Free yourself of all labels, of all distractions, and close your eyes. Become the breath in your lungs, listen for the silence, and seize your potential. Draw the blade from the forge, or add the iron-rich sand to the fire. We are malleable, shapeless, and endlessly capable of transformation.

If you don't know who you are, seek that person out. If you feel weak, seek strength. If you feel broken, seek healing. Have the courage to seek growth when you feel limited—you aren't the only one who feels shackled by the world or their circumstances. The rest of the world is hurting, too, but you must find the strength to rise above it all and find a better path. Become a student of humanity and seek to aid its progression toward freedom. Those who throw stones at you for trying to be better are shackled by an ideology of a world that told them they weren't good enough.

Prove them all wrong by living up to the weight of your expectations and no one else's.

You have no limitations.

Chapter 6

As the Midnight Frost Settles

January 27, 2023

"The most important step a man can take is not the first one, is it? It's the next one, always the next step. You cannot have my pain …I will take responsibility for what I have done, if I must fall I will rise each time a better man." –Brandon Sanderson; *Oathbringer*

 The icy air grips my lungs. Cold serenity washes over my body, taking my fear, taking my pain, and giving me clarity. The cold can sober your mind and stop a heart from bleeding out. The ice callouses over me and the man that I once was.

 It's midnight, nearly a full moon, and ten degrees outside. Most people in this community are asleep or headed off to bed, but for me, the work has just started. The end of the accounting quarter looms behind me, a testament to long hours and relentless dedication. Yet amidst the chaos, I carve out time for reflection. Busy lives offer no excuse for neglecting our purpose. The game may grow harder, but strength lies within us, waiting to be unleashed.

You always have more strength than you realize. When the weight of the world is pressing down on you, you must stand up, even if you have to crawl to your knees, scraping against rock and earth. You must get up; don't let the weight crush you, and don't surrender to your exhaustion.

I fear being called in for the post-mortem examination of my dreams. I refuse to accept the death of my ambitions, and I refuse to look at that version of myself and say, "Yes, that's him," while standing over the body. A reality where my passion has died and been replaced by "realistic" expectations is the greatest lie I can permit to enter my life.

For those peers of mine who have lost that spark, for my mother, for my brothers, and for my honor, I will continue to toe the line for those that have slackened their grip on what their reality can be. I will carry the weight of the dreams they left on the ground and continue to push forward to show them that they weren't wrong to believe.

Life can kick you in the teeth and knock you down, but you have to pick yourself up and fight for your life. Passivity, complacency, or surrender are not viable options, yet some people stay down and wait for the beating to stop. We cannot afford to turn a blind eye, and we cannot afford to be victims of the world. Instead, we need to keep shoveling coal into the forge despite our bruised bodies, despite the inevitable future beatings, and despite the words of those telling us to just lie down and take the hits.

I am a mindless beast of burden whose eyes have glazed over in the pursuit of my ambitions. The pain of failure gnaws at my heels, the weight of my dreams is a heavy load on my back, and the path ahead is more arduous than the path behind me; yet one step at a time, I choose this. I'd rather suffer for my ambitions than be comfortable in mediocrity.

As the new year rolled in, I slowly found a new breath of wind within me. December 27 marked four months since my marriage ended, and January 27 now marks five. The new year presents an opportunity to leave the past in the past and strive toward a new future. I have not overcome the sense of grief that lurks within me; however, I have put some mileage in between myself and that feeling. I haven't looked back since the day I left my old home. I haven't reached out to her once, and I won't. That part of my life, nearly six years, is buried in the year behind me.

However, even in the depths of misery, I am wired for solutions. I've slowly been building and digging myself out of the hole. The only way out of hell is forward. The only option is to keep moving forward. My mind knows the truth my heart has not yet accepted, "I will love again, I will heal, and I will grow from these experiences." My mind has finally prevailed over my heart, and I can see and think clearly.

I decided to form a new ethos for myself:

- Accept yourself as you are, then extrapolate into what you can be

- Do not close your heart off to love, and love will find its way to you

- Make yourself the priority, and see what you are capable of

- Do not compromise on what you want

With this mindset, I have set the following goals:

- Publish my second book in 2024

- Achieve my peak physical form

- Focus on my investments to replace my income

- Travel with a sense of wonder

- Connect with more people in a meaningful way

I have been experiencing physiological consequences from the depression that took a grip on me. My energy has been inconsistent, my sleep has been poor, my drive has been fluctuating, and it's been a constant tug-of-war between my heart and mind. However, at no point have I accepted these feelings as "true." This feeling of depression would have me believe that I am a failure, that nothing matters, and that I should stop trying. It wants me to lie down and lick my wounds. It wants me to disassociate from reality, to not be here, to not accept what happened, but I'm stronger than that, even when at my weakest. As the curtain draws on my vision and depression swoops in to take me, I punch through the blackness and onto the stage.

This is the audition: "Who do you want to be?" a voice calls from beyond the stage.

"Have you reached your limit?" another voice calls to me from the seats.

In my heart, I feel the ache of the loss, and I feel the wind blowing through the cracks of the broken windows to my soul.

"Is that...it?" I think to myself.

Am I just the shell of the person that I once was, a ghost clinging on to the version of myself that envisioned more?

No, "this" is not it. I need to pull deep from the well of determination within me and carve the path forward. I have seen this story many times: the hero's journey. I've always admired those who choose strength in the face of defeat. I've been brought to tears listening to those stories of people who tried just one more time despite being devasted over and over again and despite facing the absolute cruelty and despair of this world. If they can do it, why not me? We are all just characters living out our stories, and we can be all that we want to be. We need only seize the consciousness to focus, set the goal, and move forward.

In the blank canvas of my mind, I do not see "emptiness." I see limitless potential. We can choose to be the authors of our own stories or try to live by someone else's narrative.

We truly are the summation of all we think we are, and we become all that we are determined to be. The reason why those stories bring me to tears is because I feel it in my soul—that cry for freedom, the cry to try one more time.

"Fight"

"One more step"

"Fall down seven times, stand up eight."

The treasures we seek are often closer than we realize, and the distance towards them appears to be far, but the truth is, we already have all that we seek inside of us. We are the mines filled with precious ore. We must pull our greatness out from within ourselves. We must hammer, sweat, toil, and agonize over saving that person within, buried beneath layers upon layers of doubt, failure, and defeat.

When I initially, went through my divorce, there was talk of going through my "villain arc," but I realized that villains are just heroes who failed to rise above their failures. They are people who fail to keep developing, and oftentimes we become the villains in our own stories. Don't lose yourself to the pain, and don't lose the true essence of who you are. Love no matter how much it hurts, and believe no matter how many times you fail. Stand up no matter how many times you fall! Rise over and over again! Seven times? Eight times? Fifty times? One hundred times? One thousand times? The number doesn't matter; all that matters is that you have 1 more time in you.

You are the one who put those layers you have to break through there. Life is not happening to you; it happens in the way you choose to respond to events. External stimuli can only *influence* what is internal to you. Your life is not determined by external forces, but by the depth of your internal drive and your desire to succeed despite the obstacles. Don't succumb to the villain arc; remain kind, grow, heal your wounds, and give yourself time. Time is the only true measure of distance. The road to your healing starts as soon as you are ready to change.

We can grow from what we once were. Time is growth; you cannot remain the same, you can only move forward. Drag your feet, whinge, and moan, but regardless of it all, you will be forced forward, so isn't better to move in harmony with time rather than fight against it while clinging to the past? We cannot change the past; we can only learn from it, or be cursed to inevitably make the mistake again.

It's grueling work, but it must be done. Do not be afraid; you put those layers there to protect yourself from the pain of it all, but you are no longer that child, and you are no longer that person. As long as tomorrow comes, you can be reborn. Seize the reigns of your life from complacency, grasp the pickaxe, swing it high, and save yourself from the avalanche of a lifetime of rumble. You must open your mind to the possibility that perhaps you were wrong in your reason to stop. Your life is so precious. Don't be ashamed, don't fear your past, make peace with it, and go forward.

The peace you need can be found in stillness. Reach out for the void within you through mediation. You are the master of your mind, your body is your domain, and you are not subject to it, it is subject to you. Face your cowardice and your excuses. Oddly enough, I have met many people who say they "can't meditate" or they "don't feel it." If you approach things expecting failure, you will find failure.

Change your expectations, focus your intention, and you shall produce the outcome you desire. If you want to believe that you are helpless and incapable of mastering the domains of your mind, body, and spirit, you are right. Stop surrendering your power to others, step into your power, and imagine the possibility that maybe, just maybe, if you tried and believed in yourself, you could make a positive change.

Just find ten minutes in your day, sit down, close your eyes, and pour the contents of your mind out into the ether.

Let it all out of you, and empty your cup so that it can be filled again with something new.

Close your eyes, breathe deeply, one…two…three…four…five, and exhale, one…two…three…four…five. Loosen your jaw, relax your shoulders, and maintain an upright posture. Synchronize your heart and mind with your breath. First, find that feeling of nothingness—you are just a being that exists on a piece of rock propelling through the vastness of space. You are completely insignificant in the grand scheme of the universe and, by extension, so are your problems. You are small, and they are even smaller. They are just subatomic little particles floating in your headspace, dust that needs to be cleared from the bookshelves. Let it all go, let it all slip into the void.

Now in your calm, connect with the fire in your soul. What color do you see? Is it small, or is it big? Is it smoldering, or is it blazing? It can never be extinguished, not until the day you die. The embers burn and wait for a breath of life. Speak the words and be born again. Breathe again, live again, try again, and take the next step. Have the courage to heal. You decide what you are and no one else. Free yourself from the judgments of others and your own critical, negative self-talk. Remember how capable you are, and remember the moments when you were proud of yourself. You are you—you have forgotten that, but we are all capable of finding the things that we seek. Find yourself again, over and over, until you find the version of yourself that is ready for the journey ahead. Then, along the journey, discover the deeper facets of your character, the inner workings of you. Expose yourself to new things, remove yourself from small thinking, and extrapolate into infinity.

Now, come back to yourself with this new understanding. See solutions instead of problems. Only time and effort separate you from your goals. You have the time to change but be sure to set that intention.

This feeling in your heart, the one that can bring you to tears—that's you. It's the purest version of you, the one that still believes. Let that person live again. Bear the weight of it all, but this time, lift with your legs. Dig into the earth with your feet planted firmly and rage against it all. Cling to life, seize your strength, and just don't let it all be in vain.

Priming your mind and spirit is only the first step in all of this; now you need to act. Seek your physicality and carve the person you are out of the marble. You need to start directing your mental energy into physical development and prove to yourself that it is true, you can direct your life through conscious effort.

I've found my "why" again, and it's that "I need to achieve the best version of myself so that I can create the greatest amount of good possible in the world."

Many people preach, but very few do. I want to be of the class of people that do. I will do more than what is expected, and I will do more than I expect from myself. You can speak your ideals, but it is more important to live by them. Living by your ideals is proof that they can serve others as well. If your own words don't inspire you to take action, how will they inspire anyone else?

I have to do it because I know I am capable of it. I will forever regret not trying harder and not giving it my absolute all if I don't start the work today.

I started forming my protocol and mindset based on the knowledge that I have accumulated over the years. People like Wim Hof, Joe Rogan, Andy Frisella, Jocko Wilink, and Paulo Coelho have taught me the lessons I needed to progress. First things first, you need to develop your grit. Grit is the combination of tenacity and discipline. Change is hard. It is very hard. You are alchemizing your person into something new. You have all it takes inside of you to change but perhaps not the "know-how."

You begin building your discipline by cleaning. I want you to literally clean the space you sleep in, even if it is a small room and even if you think it is clean. You need to clear the clutter, and in doing so you will clear the stagnant energy around you. Once you have cleaned your room, clean your mind and clear the clutter from the shelves. You don't have to do it all at once, but you need to start. The first step to clearing your mind is to believe this one thing: "I am a capable person, and I am capable of creating the changes I set my mind to."

It is that simple, but also that hard. There is a lot of work that comes with believing in yourself, but you need to do it. Do not give yourself the option to doubt your abilities.

Limiting beliefs stem from negative self-talk, and this will affect your results. There is a concept that exists called the "Placebo Effect." In essence, it is documented scientific proof of "mind over matter." The way you think about something alters the reality around and within you. For example, it is not uncommon that during the clinical trial of a new drug, there will be at least two groups of people, an experimental group, and a control group. The purpose of the control group is to set a baseline for the experimental variable being tested.

However, in the control group, the test subjects are not given the real drug, but are instead given a sugar pill. This is something that does not contain the drug at all, but the control group is told that it does contain it. Oftentimes people in the control group will note that they are feeling better or worse from taking a pill that does nothing. This is because in their minds, they are convinced that they have taken the real thing, and what do they know about medicine? "It cures the disease" or "it has negative side effects." Belief is the melodrama of the mind; it will influence the outcome of actions that you take.

This logic makes me think of the concept of "beginner's luck." Most of us have heard the term before, meaning that when you do an activity for the first time, you are likely to succeed. It is also a reasonable justification for others to use when someone who is not as experienced as them succeeds despite the lack of skill. I have been thinking about this a lot lately. I have had moments when it felt like beginner's luck.

For example, I shot a handgun for the first time a few weeks ago at a bank when I decided that I needed some seed money for my entrepreneurial pursuits. Writing books hasn't really been paying the bills, and fitness is a long road to success. I smashed in the door, disarmed the alarms, and, in the words of Danny Devito, "I just started blasting." Needless to say, it was a flawless heist, and I am sitting pretty in Costa Rica drinking Mai Tais.

Okay, I bet you weren't expecting this plot twist! "I thought this was an inspirational book?" No, no, this is a heist, I've stolen the money, and now I'm here to steal your hearts...

Okay, back to being serious.

I went to the range and was instructed on how to shoot for the first time with a pistol expert. She taught me how to ascertain which eye was my dominant eye and how to chamber the bullets, hold the gun, and maintain a proper stance when firing. Upon my initial run of shooting, I was able to hit a perfect bullseye and other effective shots with a decent grouping on my target. She was impressed that I was able to shoot so well for my first time and then challenged me to try to hit a headshot. I calmed my mind, looked at my target, and said to myself, "Focus, and fire." I successfully placed three bullets dead center in the head on my target. She remarked that given some additional practice, I could shoot as an expert as well.

This circumstance honestly fascinated me, and I have analyzed it quite a bit. How is it that a total beginner can shoot like an "expert" with no formal training? Is it all as simple as luck?

I think the answer is a little more complicated than that. I think we can perform reasonably well the first time we attempt something because of two reasons:

1. We do not know what we are capable of and want to find out

2. Although we do not know the subject well, we want to succeed and believe it is possible

Then, due to an uninhibited mind and the belief in the possibility of success, we hit our target, bowl a strike, or win a game. Those around us chalk it up to dumb luck, but I think it may be similar to "flow state." You can enter this state of mind when you are free of doubt and filled with determination. However, we struggle to maintain a flow state mainly due to our turbulent internal worlds and those around us who anchor us down, away from our potential with their words.

Sure, your first bowl or shot may have been perfect, but then the thought protrudes in your mind: "I'll never do that again, how the hell did I manage that?"

Were you thinking that before, when you tried for the first time? No, you weren't, all you were thinking was, "Let's try, let's see what I can do. Maybe I'm good at this."

Despite our age, at any point in our lives, our minds can be childish and undeveloped. As soon as we are not sure about something, we devolve into children who don't know their worth. We wait for validation to tell us that we are good enough. We have been programmed to seek our validation externally from school and authority. We get sucked into these cookie-cutter assembly-line models of performance. We only receive validation or praise from external forces based on the quality of our work and not so much the effort put into it. Our creativity bleeds out of us as we are taught that there are only the following options: A, B, C, D, or, for the masochist AP students out there trying to prove themselves, option E, or perhaps A and E and not C, or B and D and not A, or perhaps none of the above. Your value is determined by a number two pencil and some bubbles on a scantron.

From there, your potential is assessed, and your guidance counselor will tell you if you are better off applying to a private college, community college, trade school, or sales job. If you don't fit into any of those categories, military recruiters will prey on those who don't fit in anywhere with a pull-up bar and some t-shirts. That's not to say that the military cannot provide discipline and structure to your life when you likely have none at that age.

From the moment we participate in society, we are measured, assessed, and pushed into a certain direction because someone else has determined that is where we will fit best. Even if you are a high performer who thinks they are choosing the path to their goals, odds are, you have been guided there. The herd has been culled, and you have been told that you are the best of them. "The world is your oyster, and all the possibilities are yours for the taking!"

Then, in one form or another, you are shipped off to your next re-education center to learn how to best serve as a cog in that machine. Although this next center of programming is different, you seek the structure you have been taught to fit into, and you easily fall into line. It's an old habit, a new place, but the same old, same old. You study for your tests, you compete with your peers, and then it's time to find that job. All your years of school have been building up to this moment, and you have finally made it! A great success, first in your family! You lock down that big four accounting firm job, you become a CPA, PHD, MD, RN, JD, programmer, mechanic, police officer, etc.

At first, you are excited; you finally made it, and you put on that suit or uniform with pride and excitement for the future ahead. Sure, you are working 60 hours a week because the 40-hour work week is for uninspired losers, but that's just the cost of the American dream. You have debt ranging from 10–300k from student loans because of the "quality" of the education you received, but that's okay, surely your job will pay you enough money to pay it all off! That's what you've been taught, after all. The system works, and there could not be anything possibly wrong with it!

After a few months, you're tired, but after a few years, you've settled in nicely to that "reality" your parents, teachers, and friends have always been talking about. You look back on that younger version of yourself, that kid, and chuckle at how naive they were. "Ah remember the days when you thought it just took a little hard work to change the world."

Things are starting to get serious with your significant other, and you think, "Maybe I'm ready to settle down. I couldn't do it, but maybe the next generation can. I'm too old for these dreams, I can't afford them, and I have bills to pay and a mortgage."

Sorry, I misspoke—I meant rent. You have rent to pay, and it only costs about 50–75 percent of your monthly salary. Maybe that rent will go up by $200 next year, or $600, who knows! Such is life, a box of chocolates.

Before you know it, you're 30 and settled down. Perhaps you have kids on the way, or perhaps you're freaking out because you aren't settled down and don't have kids on the way.

The years seem to have just flown by; you can't believe high school was more than 10 years ago, and college, wow, that's almost 10 years, too. You've had your head down grinding away at your job, only to surface for a quick gasp of air on the weekends, assuming your job doesn't require you to work those, too. You are part of a "big family" after all, and sometimes YOU have to make sacrifices for that family that can fire you at a moment's notice with no warning at all. So maybe you didn't get that breath of air this weekend. Perhaps you can hold it a little longer for the next weekend. Perhaps those 10 days off a year and three sick days will be enough to hold you over in between, assuming you even get that much. If you're a contractor, "God bless ya."

What if you feel sick and tired all the time, though?

Well, in that case, head over to your local pharmacy. Take some pills and caffeine and power through! You aren't of much use to the machine if your cog is too rusted to turn. You need to be productive or you have no value at all. If you can't keep up with the volume without burnout swooping in, well, that's because you are just stupid and not good enough. You need to sacrifice more! There is no balance; if you want to progress, give all of yourself to your job. If you don't, someone else will, and they will even ask to work even more than 60 hours a week because that is for uninspired losers! They will work 80 hours a week, every free second they have, and they will agonize over every minute detail that you missed!

The new year rolls in once again, and you have maybe a couple hundred or thousand in your bank account, not a lot, but just enough to maybe pay all your bills and buy some fast food. Don't worry next year will be different! You'll get that raise, maybe you'll apply for a new job, maybe things will change, maybe you might do "this," and you're thinking about doing "that."

You're always thinking about doing those things, but then your friends and family are always so kind to reel you back into your reality. They keep you grounded and remind you that there is a lot of risk in doing this or that, and instead, you should just keep doing what you are supposed to. They tell you the odds of failure are so high that it just isn't even worth trying! Perhaps this year you are tired of hearing that, and you just try it anyway! Yet although you may try that one time, you will fail. At that moment of failure, your friends, your family, your boss, your bills, and your debt will remind you that they warned you that this would happen. You see the foolish error of your ways, put your head back down, and get back to the grind!

Ah, life, it's so much simpler than I thought. The years will continue to peel away as you grind away at your job. You're 40 now, 50, 60, 70? When are we supposed to retire again? I forget.

Well, you did it! It all happened so fast! I remember being in a rush to be 13 so that I could be a teenager, basically an adult. Those years always seemed so far away, yet now, 13 years is nothing, gone in the blink of an eye. On your last day of work, you get a neat little card that everyone in the office signed, and they even scraped together a hundred bucks for you. How kind of them. The age of gold watches has long since passed, but this is nice, too. Now it's time to kick back and enjoy the fruits of your labor. Ah, but those fruits are oddly smaller than you thought they would be and not quite as sweet.

Well, you gave life your best shot. You took a risk that one time, and you failed. You tried, so there is nothing to worry about. You don't have any of those deathbed regrets because you always tried your hardest. You dared to think about things and to think about doing things! It's pretty heroic that life ended up like this; it is noble to try and fail. It is noble to understand your limitations and then live your life accordingly. So many people never find their limitations, but you did, and you stayed there! Good for you! What a wild ride life has been.

Then, BAM! A cold sweat comes down your brow, and you feel a sharp pain from your arm to your chest.

Maybe now you'll get to die and go to heaven where everything is perfect. That's where the real reward is, death. You can finally get some of that well-deserved rest and be happy there, perhaps.

Nope, just a false alarm, it was a heart attack but wasn't "the" heart attack to finish the job. Speaking of jobs, your savings didn't plan for this new medical expense, and you don't want to be a burden to your family. Perhaps it's time to get back to work—there are always bills to pay and just never enough money.

However, you'll figure it out. You always figure it out somehow. Just a little farther to go.

That's the direction your life is going in, plus or minus a few divorces, a few good moments in between, and moving a few times.

Perhaps that isn't your direction; maybe you picked yourself up by the bootstraps, no opportunities were provided to you, you worked for everything you got, and now you successfully climbed the corporate ladder somewhere. You hold some title of significance to you, one that makes your email signature just a little more important than everyone else's. The salary you make is pretty nice, and you have a nice home, 2.5 kids, and that car you always wanted.

Even if you are "successful" in terms of how much money you make, are you happy and free?

That's just the only thing that matters to me. Maybe that doesn't matter to you, and if so, I'm so sorry you had to sit through my little rant there. I hope your career continues to flourish and you get that bonus, a new car, or that raise. I hope that you get all that you deserve at your company, and your life blooms beautifully.

Personally, I can't handle reporting to someone else. I don't like someone else having control over my livelihood. I don't like being told how much I need to work and how I need to complete the work. I hate when the lines between work and life get blurred and how the term "after hours" has become utterly meaningless. What would happen if you lost that job that pays you so well today? It's 5 pm on a Friday, and you have suddenly been called in. You weren't expecting this development, and your last performance report was glowing, but the company has hit some dire straights. They are going through a corporate restructuring to counteract the turbulent economy, and you just didn't quite make the cut.

Sure, you have dedicated the last 10 years of your life to this company. Sure, you lived and breathed its company values, and sure, you sacrificed all of your personal life to fulfill the obligations of this demanding role. However, it is as the saying goes: "C'est la vie," "such is life."

Looking back on it all with the perspective of the end, I am sure you don't have a single regret. I'm sure you fully accept that you missed your kid's baseball game, those nights out with your friends, that special someone who you were enamored with but who thought you were just a workaholic. Your social life, your relationships, your physical health, your mental health, your spiritual health, your rest, your balance, your time, your freedom...those were all worthy sacrifices to the cause.

Despite losing your job today, you no doubt have acquired the skills that will make you appealing to any employer! You are a catch if you were the VP, or Director, or whatever of wherever you were at, so surely you can pull in that same big salary as before—as well as that "unlimited PTO" that you never really used and a health insurance plan to cover your blood pressure, anxiety, and depression medications. Surely you are not going to be undercut by desperate college grads willing to work at roles far beyond their current skillset at half the price of what it would cost for you.

You're not quite as young as you used to be, but undoubtedly you still have enough stamina to compete with these kids. You've sacrificed everything once already, and now you have nothing to lose! Build it all up again from the bottom. It'll be worth it. At least, at the end of the day, you have all those loved ones in your life that you can turn to during these difficult moments. Maybe now you have time to go grab that drink, play that game, or, hell, even take the dog out for a long walk. Then again, maybe your friends stopped drinking and playing games a few years ago because they got married and had kids. At least your dog is still there for you—your trusty companion, always there for you, always swooning with love and affection for you.

"When did their face get so white?" you think to yourself.

"Wow, has it been 10 years, my little fur child? How about we go for a walk? Would you like that, buddy?" Your little love is not quite as spry as they used to be, and you see they struggle to get to their feet just a little. They move just a little slower than you remember, but you leash them up anyway and just start walking! You take the same route you guys always walk, but today at the halfway mark, your friend just plops down and takes a seat.

"C'mon buddy, let's go, this is your favorite walk! We are going to the park, I'll even buy you an ice cream like we always do."

Despite your little temptations, it just seems that going further is simply out of the cards. Your pup is just too tired to make this trek…

Time just slips away so fast. Where did it all go? When did I blink? I thought if I worked hard now, I would be able to enjoy life later.

Ultimately, there is always a cost. Sometimes we just don't realize how much things truly cost, those pesky hidden fees.

You found a different void, a void of meaninglessness. Everything you ever dreamed of, gone in a blink of an eye, and you lost so much more than what you could see. You just weren't focused on those leaks in your boat, and now here you are, sinking the bottom.

Only one question remains: will you go down with the ship, or are you going to start swimming to shore?

Going down with the ship is the noble thing for the captain to do and is certainly much easier than swimming. What if you failed? What if there was no salvation and just another problem to solve? You're better off just not trying at all, just surrendering and accepting your fate.

You owe it to yourself to contemplate a life for yourself that is more than simply satisfactory. Big paycheck, fancy car, wife and kids, or not...what is true happiness to you? What have you always wanted to do? What have you always wanted to be?

Our life is far too beautiful of a phenomenon to live so complacently. Don't allow yourself to be crushed by the burdens or desires of the mundane and frivolous. You are so much more than the car you drive, the house you live in, or an email signature. You were born a living miracle, one in roughly 100 million, and those are roughly your odds for winning the first race in life. Despite the odds of it all, you are here right now. Don't squander your victory; you were quite literally born a winner. Funny, but true.

Unplug from everything and sit in the silence of your mind. You need to slow down and to access where you are in life. What went wrong? What went right? What could be better?

People often wish to go back in time and change one small decision here or there. If they did, their life would be completely different from what it is right now. However, by that same logic, have you considered that your life could be drastically different because of something small you changed today?

All we have is today; don't cling to your past or you will be dragged forward by time. We are no longer children; we cannot afford to throw tantrums and avoid accountability. Your life is yours, and what you do with it is entirely up to you.

Limiting beliefs crumble in the face of possibility. The placebo effect of belief shapes our reality, unlocking hidden potential. The concept of "beginner's luck" reveals the power of uninhibited minds free from doubt.

Society's expectations confine us, dictating our path with narrow parameters. Yet I refuse to be a cog in the machine. Success is not measured by titles or wealth, but by happiness and freedom.

As the years slip by, I refuse to succumb to complacency. The corporate ladder may offer stability, but it cannot fulfill the soul. Happiness lies in pursuing passions, not paychecks. I reject the notion of sacrificing life for work, and I am opting instead to live fully on my own terms.

Change is inevitable, but growth is a choice. I choose to embrace the unknown, to forge my own path. In the end, it is not the destination that defines us, but the journey we undertake.

Chapter 7
A Steel Thread of Will

February 13, 2023

As time progresses, the pain of the past doesn't change, you do.

You don't stop loving people even if they break your heart, and that can cause some inner conflict.

Lately, the thought of her pours through the membrane of my calloused heart. I find myself smiling when I think of good times in between; however, then I am met with the void of that past time. My love ran deep, but I blocked even the thought of her out of my head this whole time. It seems that I am no longer capable of hiding behind that mental wall. Flashes of our times together and our antics come at the most random or quiet moments. I think I'm finally starting to slow down. This is enabling me to reconcile this piece of my life.

In this reflection, I've come to understand the essence of unconditional love—not in the romantic sense, for that chapter is forever closed, but rather in the profound acceptance and forgiveness I harbor within. Despite the trials we faced, I would tread the same path again, albeit perhaps with greater insight. Alas, we cannot rewind time to apply the lessons learned; we must carry the weight of our choices and trust in our capacity to evolve.

Amongst the myriad memories, one particular recollection stands out: an ordinary evening when we returned from the gym craving German mini pancakes.

She looked over to me and said, "Wow, I really want German mini pancakes, but it takes an hour for the yeast to rise." We both paused at the bottom of the staircase that led to our apartment and looked at each other with mischievous little grins. I said, "Only an hour, you say?"

Despite the hour-long wait for the yeast to rise, our impulsive spirits propelled us up the stairs, giggling like carefree children. Ah, the liberation of adulthood, where whims are indulged without restraint.

This simple yet cherished memory evokes conflicting emotions: joy intertwined with sorrow, creating a poignant tapestry of reminiscence. At 27, I realize the youthfulness still coursing through my veins, a stark contrast to the mental aging forced upon me by a tumultuous upbringing. Survival instincts, once my staunch allies, now threaten to suffocate me. There comes a point where enduring becomes futile, where surrender to self-destructive patterns is the only viable option.

Sometimes there isn't a winning solution, and your only option is to endure until better conditions ease the burden. However, now I am able and willing to surrender those instincts because they are killing me.

Things are, but are not, as complicated as we make them out to be. Life isn't happening to us, it's just happening. You are not helpless, and you don't have to go with the ebbs and flows, but you also don't need to be in fight or flight mode every day. There will come a point in time in your life when the only person that stands in your way is you—and more importantly, what you think of yourself.

Sometimes we get trapped in that state of survival, and it gives us tunnel vision. We are just so afraid of losing what we have that we focus on the problems and not the person or people around us. You are a person, not just your traumas or the terrible things that happened along the way.

You are, we are, I am, just human.

Genuinely, no one is perfect, so stop holding yourself to that standard. You don't need to be perfect to be worthy of love, you just need to be willing to love regardless of all the pain. I think true self-love is loving the person that you are, as you are, but then also reflecting.

In the reflection and introspection of who you are, feel free to explore the possibilities of who you can be.

I think that people like things to be perfect—the perfect time, place, and feeling. However, this is just a tool for procrastinating. It's a great excuse, and you can lie to yourself as well.

I think I've struggled with the idea of perfection for most of my life, unwittingly, funny enough. I was such a perfectionist that I didn't even think of myself as one because nothing I did was ever good enough for me.

When I looked in the mirror, I'd see someone who wasn't proud of their body, despite working out every day for the last 15 years. People would often compliment me, but in my eyes, I was still just not good enough. When I published my first book, my spirits were quickly dampened by criticism from others. People would point out typos or not understand what I was saying. I poured my heart into that book, but I just didn't feel proud of it. Some would say that my book was poorly written or that I had no business writing a book because I was a young kid that knew nothing.

I was crippled by perfectionism because I saw all the ways I could have done it better and agreed with the criticisms of others, that it wasn't good enough. By extension, I didn't feel like I was good enough. Growing up, I sought validation through excellence. I only ever felt loved when I was perfect, and when I fell short of perfect, I would feel the love evaporate.

I frequently felt that love was conditional. I felt constantly criticized, "less than," and small. Rage built inside of me, and I worked harder to "prove them wrong." However, there was no proving them wrong, and even when I won, I still lost. Even with apparent metrics of excellence in my grades, my athletics, and my character, I was still just a "retard." My mother was a "Tiger Mom," and she pushed the "doctor/lawyer/engineer" narrative on my brother and me. I wanted to be a doctor, perhaps in sports medicine; however, in high school, I realized that we couldn't afford to go that path, so I went with accounting instead. I was the top business student in school and took rigorous advanced placement classes; however, even when I brought home an A, if it wasn't 100%, I'd get asked, "What happened?" I was asked that so much, to the extent that I stopped reporting it to them. I would feel the most loved when I was praised for doing a good job by those with authority. I was so desperate to prove myself, and I wanted to silence their criticisms and to be someone worthwhile. I slowly started to learn that it was a losing battle and that I needed to change my tactics.

In the past, I strived to fit in the box of the expectations of others, no matter how high the bar was set. I struggled with a sense of emotional abandonment and loneliness. Loneliness isn't so much the feeling of having no one, but more so that no one was there to catch me when I fell. Sometimes it felt that the only way I could be seen was by doing more. However, even if you pursue excellence, you will be criticized.

Ironically, I was body dysmorphic about my appearance, yet at the same time, my friends would feel free to comment that I "look like a douche because of my muscles, the clothes I wear, and my overall vibe." That one always hurt, because in my heart, I see myself as someone who is deeply compassionate, and I don't think I'm braggy so much as I am ambitious. I like talking about projects I'm working on and ideas I'm exploring and just entertaining the possibilities of it all. As for the way I dress, I really don't understand, because I'm pretty modest. Ninety-nine percent of the time I'm just wearing jeans, a True Classic t-shirt, and a hat, yet because of my physical stature, that's what people think of me, apparently. It's also frequently assumed that I'm stupid just because of my physicality. In a way, it feels like I'm never quite giving off the impression I want to. In turn, this has made me more introverted and closed off over the years.

However, it is time to grow out of that narrative. We play a role in the story of our lives, and we can be whoever and whatever we want to be. It all stems from a belief; you either have thoughts that empower you or limit you. Just know that those limitations weren't set by your parents, teachers, or anyone except YOU. There is peace in surrender; however, you don't want to surrender without putting up a fight. If you accept a limitation, just be sure that you are okay with it. Don't complain, and don't hide behind a mask of victimhood. You made your choices, so live with them. Surrender can be brave, but it is often cowardly. Never surrender when it is something within your control. It genuinely exhausts me hearing the lame excuses people have for why they don't do more with their lives. *I'm also tired of my own lame excuses.*

It's time to leave introversion, the fear of judgment, the fear of failure, the fear of not being enough, and the feeling of not being enough behind. Instead, I need to embrace a mindset that empowers me. I'm not doing things anymore to compensate for perceived weaknesses. I now only do things because I genuinely love doing it, and it excites me to see progress. There is a question that gets asked on Andy Frisella's Podcasts, *REALAF* and *MFCEO*, that I like: "Do you hate losing, or do you love to win?"

I would say that I was always 50/50 on the matter. I hate losing because I hate looking foolish and failing to reach my objectives. I hate the feeling of loss and not meeting the par on something important to me. However, that is just a fear of failure, and that should not be what motivates me. Instead, I'm switching teams and doubling down on my "love of winning." I do love winning. I am competitive, I like being the best, and I like being an authority on any subject matter. It is satisfying to take on new challenges and succeed in the face of insurmountable odds. I love the feeling of exceeding my own expectations and outperforming average.

I think the thing that I really want is "freedom." Some chains are not visible to the human eye, but just because others don't see them doesn't mean they are not there. I have never felt free because I carried the weight of my expectations and the weight of others. I carried the weight of my ambitions and the weight of criticism from others. Is the weight the problem? Or am I just not strong enough?

In my divorce, although it felt like I lost everything that mattered to me, I was also set free. The chains of obligation have been removed, and now I can focus wholeheartedly on my ambitions without distraction. This is freedom, and the cost was high, but such are the stakes in life. It's an *equivalent exchange.*

I kept telling the world I wanted more and that I wanted to win, and the world rewarded me by giving me the only possible path to this goal. I needed to be able to go internally, reassess, reflect, and grow from the pain. I can survive doomsday and still find my way back to myself and grow from the experience. The people in our lives can be assets or liabilities, and I'm trying to live debt free.

What was once deep love grew into something that was emotionally compromising to me. I felt constantly emotionally exhausted when trying to cope with simple tribulations, but no matter how much effort I put in, there was no solving the problem. She needed to solve it herself, and I can't fix everyone's problems. That is something I need to accept.

Those last few months together with her really took every last drop of gas in my tank. I was completely empty, and I have no regrets. I know now that I did everything in my power to help, but I still failed. This is a surrender that I can accept because some things are just out of my control. I do still love her for everything in between and all the great moments we shared. We were once synergized, but now we are nothing.

This feeling I have discovered is "the void." The feeling of "losing" someone you loved so deeply is haunting, but it is the bitter medicine I needed. Now my view of relationships and women has changed. You can't put people on pedestals—you have to see them for who they are. The depth of your character does not matter if your partner does not honor it and match it. My standards have grown higher than before, and I'm wiser from it. Life doesn't give out too many second chances, so I'll be sure to be more careful to who I give my love and trust in the future.

The first person that deserves my love and trust is me. I have no more room for cowardice, doubt, and fear in my heart. I will no longer limit myself with negative thoughts about my capabilities, and I will not take on the emotional burdens of others unless they are equally concerned about me. I will remain free and continue to seek freedom and growth. I know this is harsh, but it is true. It's not done or thought of with any malice, just objective thought.

Don't tell me that you love me, show me.

The words "I love you" have become meaningless to me, or rather, they have lost their gravity from superficial and callous overuse. You shouldn't tell someone you love them with a little grunt of, "Love you, g'night." Instead of blurting out "love ya" when you get that little urge, let it build up inside of you. Hold it inside of you and save it for a special moment. Instead, do something that shows the other person that you love them. For most people, it is just quality time, or perhaps buying a small gift that shows them you thought of them. Personally, I felt the most loved when I was working hard on something, and she would come into my office with a coffee and a hug. It never took much.

I just don't want to be told that anymore because it is frivolous and fragile. Instead, show me that you love me. When you kiss me, kiss me deeply. When you leave, take me with your thoughts. When you're scared, come to me, and when I fall, pick me up. Love me without saying a word, and I'll do the same. If you feel compelled beyond your control to tell me, look me in the eyes and speak from your heart. Build a bridge from my heart to yours in that shared moment. Only then will I accept your "I love you." Show me the depth of your character, your strength, your dreams, your hopes, and your fears. Share all of yourself with me in trust, and I will surrender and do the same for you.

Love is a war of attrition. I will withhold until I can't, until the feeling is too strong and I feel compelled to raise a white flag to you. Trust is the final bastion of my heart. If you can earn my trust, and I can earn yours, we will be invincible. I want to share an endless, beautiful, budding growth of love together; otherwise, winter will come and kill it all. Trust is what keeps me around to tend the fields. As old things die, I have faith that new things shall come and take their place. I just want each rebirth and each incarnation of our evolution to be synchronized.

I am prepared to wait, and I'm not interested in meaningless encounters of triviality. One-night stands are not victories—they never have been, and they just take more and more of you. I'm someone who cares about people deeply, and I don't want to lose that piece of myself to vanity and bad advice. To have sex with someone is the most intimate, vulnerable, and meaningful thing you can do as a human being. It is arguably the highest expression of love we can give to another person, and it is not something we should take lightly. Of course, there are other expressions of love, but as someone who is not a father, I can say that this is the highest form I have been a part of. Although my toasted little red bean bun of a dog is my daughter, I know it will be different one day.

One-night stands can also lead to uncomfortable situations. That's perhaps my number one fear: a complete stranger calling me and telling me, "I'm late." Just the thought of that sentence makes me sweat, and many men have had at least one scare of this. Bringing a child into the world is a beautiful experience, but it is also a sacred duty. Personally, I would never want to be in that position with a stranger. *Even Drake is putting tabasco sauce to use just in case, and guess what, he was right...*the world is a scary place, and in the shadows of human character, dastardly deeds brew. When cowardice lights the fire in the human heart instead of honor, it burns down the world instead of illuminating it.

No, the cost of the freedom I have acquired was far too great, and I cannot afford to foolishly muck it up by anchoring myself down due to bad decision-making. However, I do not wish to be insensitive to some of you who may be in that situation. I empathize with your experience, and I am expressing my innate nature as a strategist. I think it is a noble burden to step up to the plate and become a parent to a child. It is a sacred duty, and no one is ever really ready for it. However, despite how difficult it is, it is a glorious pursuit to watch your little seed grow. I just fear not being a good father and not being present in my child's life every day. In order to mitigate that fear, I plan.

There is a book I have been reading slowly for a while now, *The Island of the World* by Michael O'Brien. The story follows the turbulent life of Josip Lasta from adolescence to adulthood. A pretty wonderful woman that I was dating for a little while referred it to me and said it gave her some insight when she was going through a particularly difficult time in her life. Josip's life is stained with constant agony, despair, and loss, yet it all comes to show the resilience of the human heart.

He grows up on a quiet mountainside called Rajska Polja, "The Fields of Heaven." His last name, Lasta, becomes significant with a play on words, "Lastavica." A lastavica is a type of bird, a swallow. There are times throughout the book when Josip endures so much pain and misfortune that he both loses his name or has it stolen from him. Often times, in these moments, he will refer to himself as "The Lastavica of the Fields of Heaven."

In particular, there is an instance when Josip is captured by enemy soldiers that interrogate, beat, debase, and steal every last morsel of dignity from him. He's not a soldier; he is a mathematician, a poet, and a lastavica. They take him to the "Naked Island." He is stolen away from society. His life, his freedom, his love, his hope, his name—everything is taken from him.

The guards gather the prisoners, strip them of their clothes, and make them get in the queue to play a game, "Run Rabbit." The guards line side by side and create a pathway through the middle. With their truncheons (basically nightsticks) in hand, they bark the command to brittle and broken men: "Run Rabbit!" Josip watches as the first man runs through the passage and witnesses the guards beat him to death; when the rabbit is subdued, the guards shout, "Lunch Time!" The second man in line falls to his knees, sobs, and begs the guards to spare him.

The guards look within themselves and see the error of their ways. They see the humanity in front of them, bare and naked, and change their ways. At least, that is what would have happened in a fairytale. Reality is far more cruel and disgusting. The guards, the wolves, laugh and leap forward in a maelstrom, bludgeoning the weak man. They finish the job; he accepted death before the beating, and they were the reapers.

Josip is the last in line, and it finally comes down to his turn. The cement is stained with the blood of those before him, his body already feels broken, yet, he has to keep going. The guards shout, "Run Rabbit!"

Josip charges forward, and the guards beat him to his knees and back away. They are about to finish the job, but then they see Josip struggle to rise to his knees, slipping on his own blood. The wolves see his spirit is not quite broken yet and say, "Okay! Let's make him run again, 'RUN RABBIT!'" Josip endures the fury of hell as he bears the strikes of the truncheons, barraging him on all sides. His teeth break, his ribs crack, and his body burns with pain.

Again, he has been beaten down to his knees, and he forces himself to rise again. The wolves remark, "What an ox! We can't let this one go to waste!" The wolves consider beating him down and finishing it, but another guard remarks, "No, make him run again!"

He struggles to his feet, wobbling, but standing. The guard shouts, "Run Rabbit!" They beat him badly this time, so bad that he can't stand again. Despite this, he begins to crawl forward, inch by inch, slithering through pools of blood. The wolves remark in mock amazement, "Salamander! Reptile!"

Josip wishes for death. His whole life has been nothing but agony, nothing but suffering and loss at the hands of tyrants. Yet even in his despair, his poet's heart sees himself clearly: "He is a steel thread of will dragging a sack of agony."

Another guard shouts, "Enough!"

Then he announces that, "It is time to give baby a bath." Two guards walk over and carry his limp broken body. One whispers, "Courage," to Josip, and then they proceed to dunk him head-first in a barrel of seawater that has been mixed with the blood of others before him. A bloody baptism of beastly brutality. Josip had already known agony, but now he is truly converted.

Honestly, this book constantly brings me to tears, and I can barely read 20 pages without gritting my teeth a little. I empathize so deeply with Josip and his struggles; despite the pain, despite wanting to give up, he just can't stop himself from going forward. I actually said something similar to him once in my college application essay: "As long as there is a single thread of light in the darkness, I will seize it and save myself."

Even in the darkest moments of our lives, in the bitterest of struggles and most brutal of defeats, there is always at least one single thread of hope. We can choose to surrender, lie there, and accept the darkness around us. It's easier to let go, to be swallowed by the pain, and to fade into nonexistence. Death is a welcome gift to a lifetime of suffering.

There have been times when I was almost completely swallowed by the darkness. There have been times when the world felt so unfair, cruel, and pointless that I just wanted to shed my attachments to it. It can feel like all of this is for nothing, and that we are trapped in a cycle of the frivolity.

However, even in those moments when I thought about giving it all up, I just couldn't. I'd try to close my eyes to any hope of change, a slight improvement to my circumstances, but then I'd see a spot of light trying to permeate through my closed eyes.

Head underwater, heart on the floor, and my spirit in shambles, I opened my eyes "one more time." I, too, am a steel thread of will, and I shall seize the thinnest ray of hope with two hands. Broken body or not, there is always fire in my bones. The embers just need a breath of new life and belief. The fire may weaken, but it only dies when you die. Life itself is fire, its oxygen is your intention. Seize the reigns in whatever way you can—there is a way, and there is always at least one thing you can do to improve your circumstances.

Just as Josip slithered forward, inch by inch, humiliated, devastated, broken, afraid, tired, and weak, I have that same strength within me, *as do you.*

Josip was neither an ox nor a rabbit. He was a lastavica, a lastavica of the Fields of Heaven. He survived their brutality, and he passed their sick test, but in his choice to live, he also chose to suffer. He didn't die on his knees, a coward too afraid to act. He didn't hesitate when the fangs of the wolves ripped into him; he put his entire soul, every ounce of concentration, into moving forward. He knew the only way out of hell is forward. Demons take no pity on the weak, but they do pause to observe a man that continues to rise despite their beatings. In choosing to rise again, you instill fear in those demons. Strength is a universal language, and true strength is admired by all, good or evil.

He survived the first test, but now he would be faced with a different sort of suffering. He would be treated as "less than" as they stripped him and the other prisoners of their humanity. They were just cogs in the machine, and they mined the quarry and moved the stone. If their cog failed to turn, they would be shot. He witnessed cruelty after cruelty, brutality after brutality, and yet he never surrendered the idea that he would escape and be reunited with the ones he loved most.

There eventually came a night when he saw his opportunity to escape. The bold will often find opportunities when others are afraid.

There was a terrible storm, and fierce winds raged and battered the island. The guards became more relaxed and retreated inside for fear of the storm. At this moment, Josip understood that this was the only chance he was going to get. His friends told him not to leave, that his death was certain, and that would die if he tried to leave. They told him that he is better off enduring and waiting to be rescued. Surely someone would come to save them.

That was a roll of the dice he could not afford to take, and his wings could weather the storm. He moved with stealth and tact and successfully navigated out of the camp. Yet again, he passed another test, and yet again, he was met with another beast to slay. Although the storm lacerated his flesh, stole his strength, and tested him, it was also the only thing saving him from the pursuit of the guards.

Josip has known hell, and despite its brutality, his knowledge of it is greater than others. With this knowledge that he has seen hell over and over again, he knows that he is a man that can continue to face it. Hell was his normal, and while others cowered before its wrath, he plunged through its familiar landscape because he knew that on the other side of this hell was freedom.

As for whether he made it or not? Maybe you should read the book.

As I took one final lap around the community I'd been staying at, something began to flow down my cheek.

"I'm human, and it is okay to cry," I told myself.

These weren't sad tears either, I was just so moved by the strength of this man. Although he is not a real character, he inspires me so deeply.

I'd been going through my own hell, too, long before this heartbreak. I've been broken many times by the ones that I loved, by random cruelty, and by misfortune.

I talked about a lot of my past wounds in my previous book, *The Ink of My Soul and the Fire in My Bones*. The Devil often takes root in our homes, creating a hell we are forced to return to each day. My father was mine. I have laid that devil to rest, though, and I have grown from the experience.

As the void in my house grew more apparent, I tried to step up and be "the man of the house." I tried to be everyone's strength and made it my purpose to save everyone. I wouldn't let our house crumble, and I was prepared to make whatever sacrifices necessary to be successful. I hated the way we lived. I hated feeling poor and that we were always just barely getting by. I loved my mother for everything she did to keep us afloat. It was clear that my father was the enemy and she was the good guy, but I had grown out of that thinking long ago. I understand that both my mother and my father are just people. Their traumas and how they reacted to them shaped them. No one is perfect, and by no means was I a perfect son or brother, but I take accountability for my shortcomings.

I just felt this constant pressure in my heart and skull. I felt confined by my reality, never enabled, despite having the desire to succeed and the work ethic to back it up. It hurt me to watch others get the opportunities I desired with every ounce of my being but not be able to afford them. Not having access to the same opportuniteis drove me mad with jealousy, bitterness, and anger.

I was the only one feeding my potential, and I came to accept that. I looked at my life, my environment, my bank account, and my anger. I realized that I wanted to move as far away from this person as I could. I realized no one cared if I succeeded or failed, but everyone was willing to take a slice of my cake, claiming their part in it all.

No, there were no role models for me.

I loved my father, and I love my mother, and my brother, too, but my true love was my dog, Fritz. Fritz was a grey and white mini-schnauzer. He was my best friend and my sense of peace and emotional security. He was the only one who accepted me wholly as I was, and the only one who let me cry and break. For everyone else, I had to be strong. I became so obsessed with strength, discipline, and focus that I was often filled with disgust for those who lived so carefreely. I never squandered an ounce of sympathy for those that were "too depressed or too anxious" to advance forward. I was often too hard on my brother because he just didn't see the war I was fighting alone.

I tried to appease the aggressors in my environment by curbing my emotions and soothing their turbulence. I was constantly struggling to be "left of bang." When my anger did slip, I was righteously punished by the same aggressors that anchored me down. My anger hid deeply internally, as did my other emotions. I had to seal those demons inside of me and put them to work.

I listen to "hardcore" music, which is a branch of metal, and my favorite band is Hatebreed. Their music is so powerful, filled with rage channeled into motivation. Their music lifted me up over and over again to be the best version of myself. To others, my music was just anger, but the lyrics I heard were as follows:

"Honor never dies"
"Remain steadfast. Perseverance.
Against all opposition. Crushing all limitations."
"Sometimes, standing for what you believe,
means standing alone."
"Live for this, if you don't live for something,
you'll die for nothing."
"Facing what consumes you is the only way to be free."
"Who's got more heart than you? No one!"
"Now, is the time for me to rise to my feet, wipe your spit
from my face, wipe these tears from my eyes."
"If you want to make a difference in the world,
it means you have to be different from the world you see.
Free yourself from burdens that you know exist,
don't carry the curse of the fatalist."
"Supremacy of mind. Supremacy of body.
Supremacy of spirit. Supremacy of self."
"This day is worth living, this fight is worth
fighting, this hope is worth hoping.
What I walk away from is not my master."

Where others just heard anger, I heard hope and found strength from the words. This kind of music was the only way to express myself and the depth of my passion to succeed.

When I look back at high school, there was no one that I admired. I had no celebrity that inspired me, aside from Arnold Schwarzenegger. One guy my mom dated loaned me his copy of *Arnold's Body Building Encyclopedia*. The keys to success come at unexpected times, but you must stay vigilant for these moments.

Whenever I identified a deficiency within myself, I sought to conquer it—it is that simple. My father made me feel stupid, so I worked hard in academics and took the most rigorous coursework possible. My mother wasn't satisfied unless I was perfect in my academics, so I strived for perfection.

My father made me feel as if there was no kindness in the world, so I strived to be kind to others. My mother showed me that just kindness is not enough to survive.

My father made me feel weak and small, and I was too old for my mother to protect me, so I sought strength. Ever since the fifth grade, I worked out in some shape or form. I tried to be strong, to compete with my peers physically, and to establish myself as strong, smart, and kind.

When the ninth grade rolled in, I locked myself in the weight room in my pursuit of strength. Every day after school, I either went to the weight room in my gymnasium or rode my bike to the gym I was a member of. I was so disgusted with my own weakness and my own helplessness to stand up to the violent aggression of the world around me. There was never any mercy; if I was weak, I would be devoured. I constantly felt the pressure trying to break me, and all I would hear in my head was,

> "You're weak."
> "You're pathetic."
> "You're stupid."
> "Nobody gives a fuck about you."
> "They want you to fail."
> "Prove them wrong."
> "Become strong."
> "Defeat your opposition."
> "Break yourself down, build yourself up."
> "Win at all costs."

By the end of freshman year, I could bench press 155 lbs while weighing 150 lbs. By senior year, I was 170 lbs and could press 205 lbs. There were no role models, there were only demons that I needed to kill. That's honestly all I can remember. As I would walk in the hallways, I would just imagine fire burning around me as my aura. My boiling rage and my determination just manifested in the real world by sheer force of will. I would imagine the heat to be so intense that it would melt the lockers, the floors, and the fabric of reality around me. I would blast my music in my headphones as I surveyed my environment and my hatred of it. I'd watch obnoxious and aggressive teens conduct themselves carelessly and shamelessly. They tried to assert dominance over other students with their brashness and aggression, but all I saw were little dogs trying to act big. In my eyes, they could never truly be dominant, as true dominance was found in self-mastery. They were just children, completely out of control with no bearing on their emotions. They felt the sting of cruelty at one point or another, but they learned nothing from it. If you truly know pain, you wouldn't wish to inflict it on others. Those people took the wrong side at the fork in the road. They decided to make others weaker to overcome their weakness. You should seek strength to defeat weakness and never inflict pain to make yourself feel strong.

My sense of awareness was high. I evaluated my environment and myself and formed a path forward in my mind. I seared the brush ahead of me with a will of fire, and when met with cement walls, I burned even more intensely, melting concrete, trampling obstacles, and smashing through walls of doubt.

At one point, I was a candidate for a special scholarship, "The Colonial Fund." Eight people out of my class of 756 were selected to be interviewed by former alumni for a full scholarship to the school of their choice. We each had to write an essay and present our transcripts to get through the first round, and for the final round, we were brought to the investment firm and interviewed one on one.

The night before, I had a dream that I was falling from space down to earth. I was paralyzed as I fell, and my body was engulfed by flames as I entered the earth's atmosphere. I closed my eyes in my dream and just took a breath. Just before I hit the pavement, I rapidly turned and started to fly. I often dream about flying, especially when I have lucid dreams, but this one stood out to me.

On the day of the interview, I dressed in a suit and wore my lucky tie that was part of an ensemble that was gifted to me once before. The tie was from a moment when I spread my wings when they were pinched and won several awards at a debate competition.

This day was my moment, and all my struggles meant something to me, to be here and just prove to them all that I was worthy. Someone finally saw me and how badly I wanted to be free.

One in eight, a 13 percent chance of success, *lucky numbers*. (*I know it is 12.5 percent, chill out, nerd*). We took a bus to the firm, and I was locked in and focused. I was brought into the interview, and the first thing the interviewer said to me was, "Why was your essay so angry? Also, why haven't you applied to more Ivy League schools?"

As I started to speak, I began to get a little choked up, "It's not anger...it's my fire...it's my determination. I want to succeed...I want to be successful."

Tears started to well in my eyes, and I was perplexed. I had never cried like this before. My voice felt shaky, and my body started to shiver.

"Okay, but why aren't you applying to schools like Harvard or Princeton?"

I answered and started to lose control over my emotions, "Why do you think I am good enough for that?"

He scoffed at me and said, "Look at your grades, kid, you're top of your class, all these AP classes, best debater in the state...why wouldn't you apply? Out of all the essays I read, yours was the most intense. There was so much anger that it shocked me. Where is all this anger coming from?"

Tears started to flow down my cheeks, and my facial muscles started to twitch as I spoke. "It's not...anger...it's my... fire...many people...Told me...I was...Stupid. They said... I wasn't...good enough...I wanted...to show them...they were wrong...now I am here...and just want one chance...to be successful...I want to show them...I want to help others."

He gave me a moment to compose myself and asked, "Okay, last question. Who here, other than you, deserves to win?"

I honestly anticipated him asking this question. I figured he would try to throw us off at some point with it. I already had an answer for it. "There is one other person here that really deserves to win. Her name is Erin. She has been obsessing over college prep, constantly studying, constantly taking exams, and working on her SATs. She is very ambitious and deserves a chance to succeed. However, I also want this opportunity, and I won't say she deserves it more. I can't surrender that. I've fought hard to get here, and this opportunity could change my life."

He nodded and said, "I'll give you a few minutes to compose yourself. I'll have my assistant bring some tissues."

I shook his hand, said, "Thank you for this opportunity," and apologized for crying.

He said, "No worries," and left the room.

I sat for a moment and focused on catching my breath. I was perplexed that I completely lost control of myself in this critical moment. I was a little embarrassed. Still, I accepted that "it is what it is."

We all went through our rounds, and before we knew it, we were on the bus ride back. After about a week or so, the interviewer's assistant emailed all of us and quoted his answer on the results. "When I asked you who should win other than yourself, for the most part, you all said this one person because she was kind. That made the decision clear, obviously, so I went with her."

My heart broke a little with that bitter feeling of disappointment. "I came so close, yet still fell short," I thought to myself.

It's been years since then, but I think what that experience taught me was that "no one can see what is in your heart unless you share it."

The loss hurt, but it was nothing new. I never let myself get my hopes up to spare myself from disappointment. I thought that perhaps someone had finally seen my potential as I did, but I was wrong. I was just some kid in his office that day. Even if one opportunity passes by you, there is an abundance of opportunities around you. You just need to expand your field of vision.

These shortcomings tear into our hearts. These disappointments leave scars.

However, we simply need to fill the cracks and seal them with gold. There is beauty in restoring something that has been broken. There is so much beauty in just being alive! Wear these scars with pride, my friend—they didn't kill you. You broke, but you fixed yourself again! You cannot be defeated! The pain is temporary, but the lessons we take from the experiences last a lifetime.

As I bid farewell to the demons of my past, I embrace the uncertainty of the future with open arms. For in the crucible of adversity, I've discovered the essence of my being—a steel thread of will, unyielding in its pursuit of truth and authenticity.

So, as tears of catharsis trickle down my cheeks, I embrace my humanity with humility and grace. For it's in our vulnerability that we find strength and in our imperfections that we find beauty. And though the journey ahead may be fraught with challenges, I march onward with unwavering resolve, guided by the light of self-discovery and love.

Chapter 8
THE LASTAVICA OF FREEDOM

February 28, 2023,

The day had finally come. It had been difficult to get to this point, but I finally made it.

Rather, "we made it."

I went through my checklist and took a lap around the house to make sure that I had everything. It was time to *embark* on my next journey.

I changed into some comfortable clothes, loaded my suitcase into the car, and, most importantly, checked for my passport for the tenth time. My stomach was in knots, and I could feel the tension in my face.

I had a short dialogue with myself: "Today is the day, man! Smile, for heaven's sake! You did it, you have everything, you made your list, and you checked it twice, and you know who has been naughty or nice. You are literally in the car right now headed to the one place you have been trying to reach for months. Better than that, you pulled off the impossible."

The week leading up to this moment had been ridiculously stressful and required a lot of last-minute adjustments, but I wasn't going to believe it was happening until I was on that plane.

As "the kids" are saying these days, before, "I was in Spain, without the S." However, today was the day that I finally rectified the matter and returned to the first place I ever felt free in. I can't believe it has been seven years since I was last in Spain—it still feels fresh in my mind. There is a wealth of emotion attached to this place for me, and a lot of it comes from books like The Alchemist and *For Whom the Bell Tolls*. Ever since my friend Jeff Gao—funny enough, another person I met in the fifth grade—offered me the extra room at his place, I had felt the call of the *Levanter*.

I find it truly remarkable that two people who I met when I was 10 years old ended up offering me a place as a home in my darkest hour. I still remember when Jeff called me and said, "You're not just my friend, you're my brother, and I want you to know that I want you to come here. I have an extra room and a bed for you here. Come and take some time to collect yourself, and we will have a lot of fun here. And, of course, Tsuki is welcome, too. It would be nice to have a dog in the house!"

My heart grasped onto that ray of hope. It would feel like returning home. I knew that I had to go back, and I had to take this time for myself.

Unfortunately, having Tsuki made it extremely difficult to coordinate. I had booked four separate flights to Spain since the offer was made because there was always some bureaucratic thing that made it nearly impossible for me to take her, or a general lack of useful information. There is nothing more fun than when the experts don't even know how to proceed. I called airlines and freight companies trying to figure out a way to transport the angel girl safely with me, but no one seemed to know the actual process of how to do it. This leads to a lot of conflicting information or just a general lack thereof.

I scoured Long Island for a veterinarian that could assist me with the paperwork, but honestly, no one knew what they were doing, or they just didn't want to do the extra work to figure it out. Eventually, I found one agency to work with me. They were friendly but had wildly out-of-date technologically. They struggled with the idea of emailing documents and were extremely stuck in their ways. I had to go and fax something in 2023 when I could have just emailed a PDF.

Blood dripped from my nose as I suffered from a minor aneurysm while the receptionist argued with me that sending an email was simply impossible. I was tempted to make an email account for them and revolutionize the way they did business, but I resigned and accepted that there was no convincing some people. A friend of mine says that "stress is money." He's not wrong; sometimes it is less stressful to throw money at a problem and let it solve itself. Oftentimes the little expense is just worth it in the face of the headache of trying to explain logic to another person.

If you are a fan of Brandon Sanderson, it kind of felt like the moment when Shallan was trying to start a fire in Shadesmar. She desperately tried to convince a stick that it could burn and be a fire that warmed her but was stubbornly met with the response, "I am a stick." No appeal of logic to the stick would work, and despite the overwhelming body of evidence that a stick could, in fact, become a fire, the stick simply said, "I am a stick."

Funny enough, people are like that, too. You try to tell them that they can be something, but they are just so stuck on what they are. *That's a philosophical rabbit hole for later, though.*

I successfully booked my flight with American Airlines for the fourth time and booked Tsuki with their PetEmbark service. My mother drove me about half of the way there, and then I ordered an Uber for the rest of the trek.

As per usual, the universe had some last-minute stressors for me; however, I prepared for them in the best way I could... I ALWAYS arrive at the airport early.

I spoke to the representative at the counter and was met with the sentence, "Only military personnel can travel with pets." Another classic "no one knows what they are talking" about situation.

I argued politely and explained that they had a service called "PetEmbark," and that I booked a flight today. I simply need to drop off my dog for her reservation. She continued to argue with me, but then someone else intervened and let me know I had to bring her to the freight building. When I asked for directions, I was met with five-star customer service and was told to "Google it."

Awesome.

It's okay, we are going to pull this off today, Ethan. Just stay calm, you are here to board your flight. These are just things that are happening, and they don't need to ruin my emotions. Face the problems with sound logic. Don't react emotionally, react logically. Simply see the facts and then find solutions.

I trudged on out of the terminal with my large luggage, carry-on bag, and a carrier with Tsuki in it. I was a certified mini-U-Haul truck desperate to make my move. I called yet another Uber and sobbed quietly as I paid $25 for a 10-minute drive to the freight building.

Funny enough, the driver only spoke Spanish, so it felt like a warm-up exercise as I recounted the subtle differences between "derecho" and "derecha."

I arrived at the facility confident that all my paperwork was in order. I had called beforehand to ensure that I had everything I needed to get on this flight.

That was my first mistake. The art of war is founded on deception.

I was told that my APHIS certification, a literal USDA certification that required a health certificate to get, was not sufficient. I was told to get yet another health certificate, and I only had a few hours to do it.

DEEP BREATH. LOGIC, USE LOGIC!

"Okay, do I have enough time to get it now? Is there a location nearby where I can get it?" I asked.

"Yes, it's good that you got here early ..."

I smirked to myself, ALWAYS early. *Insert deep breath emoji*

"There is a facility down the street. It is within walking distance, and you can get a new health certificate there."

"Perfect, a solution," I said.

This one-man U-Haul picked up the precious cargo and lugged her over about 800 meters to the vet. At this point, I explained my situation and was promptly met with a freshly printed piece of paper that cost $250. Before, it was $75, but there is nothing like taking advantage of customers when they are in a difficult situation! People warned me about getting scammed in Europe, but I was getting robbed blind in America. Tsuki never left her crate for an evaluation—she only left to get pet by everyone for a few minutes.

Had I known that they were going to gouge me, I would have charged them for petting fees, or perhaps instructed Tsuki to bite their greedy little fingers off.

I made my way back to the freight facility and met the receptionist with an exhausted smile of victory.

In my head, I heard Kratos from the *God of War* franchise shouting, "DO YOU SEE GODS OF OLYMPUS?! DO YOU NEED MORE PROOF THAN THIS?!"

My wallet was bleeding out, and my window of opportunity was closing, but with this paper, I delivered the final decisive strike.

Tsuki was finally all squared off. I put her lucky red jacket on, fluffed her blankets and pillows, and kissed her on the head as I handed her off.

With an enormous sigh of relief, I headed back to the terminal and met the receptionist with my luggage. I might as well have been covered in dirt with my clothes torn, I felt so ragged. However, I just needed to get past this final wall to get on my plane.

My luggage went on the scale: 49.5 lbs.

I shed a solitary tear of gratitude as I bowed my head to the gods for the eight ounces of grace they afforded me by not being over the 50 lbs limit. I made my way through security and the incredibly rude TSA officers. I always marvel at how rude people choose to be when politeness is free, but alas, a stick is a stick.

I crawled to the finish line after months of coordination, failures, and trials, but then made a sudden left turn when I saw a sports bar. I sat down at the high-top table, cringed at the $30 burger, but said, "Fuck it," and even got a beer.

AH, $40 for a burger and a beer, now this is FREEDOM!

Perhaps it's because it's Valentine's day? Damn, I'm just so romantic for taking myself to Spain, so beautiful.

After a few hours longer of waiting, I was finally boarding my plane to where I would be spending the next three months of my life. As I went down the aisle to my seat, I saw there was an abuelita that was occupying my window seat. I sighed and asked her if she prefers the window—*in Spanish*—and out of the kindness of my heart, I yielded it to her. My kindness was later rewarded when she gave me her "Strofehahaha" wafer cookie, or however you spell that. Once again, the scales of Karma were balanced!

If Josip is the Lastavica of the Fields of Heaven, perhaps I am the Lastavica of Freedom? It was time for me to take flight, spread my wings, and swim in the vast open sky above me. To feel free is perhaps the only thing I ever wanted. In some ways, I know I am free, but in others, it all feels like an illusion, a lie I have to tell myself to keep pushing forward.

I won't let it be a lie, though; the freedom I seek can be achieved. I don't care about all the material things—I could give 2 shits about designer labels or how fancy my car is.

None of that matters, and it ultimately contributes to our slavery to our things. I don't have the excess to justify such frivolous expenditures; all excess of mine will be invested over and over and OVER again until it sets me truly free. My salary at my job is good, but what is the cost? Twelve-hour days, no paid overtime, and every quarter all my freedom is taken from me as I am required to work every weekend. When did the lines get so blurred? Whatever happened to balance? The problem is, we accept that this is simply what is required of us. We are paid for 40 hours but work 60 or 80 hours. Then, at the end of the month, we only have a little money left over despite working basically two jobs.

We are just too afraid to bite the hand that feeds us. We are too afraid to express logic to those in charge because we know that there is no voice. There is no rationalization, and all that matters is productivity. Slave away until you die, and your death will not be mourned—it will merely be an inconvenience at best.

After taxes, I make around $6k a month, but even that just doesn't feel like enough. Everything is just so expensive, it feels like the price of freedom goes up faster with inflation every year as opposed to my salary. Financial alchemy requires blood sacrifices; it is the only equivalent exchange. I give my arms, my legs, my heart, my soul, and everything in between just for a chance to breathe fresh air again, to be uninhibited by it all. These jobs just chip away at us, scraping our edges away and forcing us into a mold. Creativity dies a little more every day that we fail to take action.

I've made a plan to endure, and that is my greatest strength. Endurance comes from discipline. I can endure the suffering and sacrifice because in the distance, I can see freedom. The only thing that stands between us is time. Rather than making payments, I see investments. Each investment I make is a step toward that future, to freedom. Once I solve it, I swear I'm going to find a way to help others out of this hell as well. Rather than spending a million dollars a month on wine or $50k on a watch, I'm going to build systems that enable people and that are also profitable to me. An investment can also serve a community, a true trickle-down economy.

I want to build the blueprint to freedom, to find the path unseen that is hidden from our vision. One of my dreams is to build beautiful tiny home communities with affordable rent so that people actually have a fighting chance of breaking out of the system. Then I'll outline a path to success for others to follow that starts at $0. We need seed money before we can enjoy any fruits of our labor. I have some outlines in my head to show people ways they can make more money that are relatively simple, but I want to streamline this process. I'm slowly seeing the building blocks of my life stack together, but I know that with each decision I make, I am forming the foundation of something greater.

I want this next year to be different, for you, and me. The only way I see forward is through grueling sacrifice. I'm going to figure this out for all of us; freedom should be shared, not greedily hoarded away. Some people have so much power and influence, yet all they do is line their pockets. There is no community, and there is no representation, just avariciously vicious people serving their self-interests.

I promise that when I make it out of this hell, I'm coming back with a ladder to get you all out. My dream is to teach people what they need to learn to be free. To teach something, we must first understand it, and accomplish it. For now, all I can do is start the conversation, but let's start thinking. Put all the emotion to the side, use logic, and face the fear in the pit of your stomach. Look at your finances no matter how much it stresses you out and begin your escape plan.

I didn't sleep much on the flight, only for a brief two hours, since my mind was racing with excitement, nervousness for my dog, and curiosity for the possibilities and opportunities in front of me. Before I knew it, I landed in Madrid, a familiar sight, and one that filled me with some hope. I thought, *I'm about to enter a truly beautiful time in my life.*

I navigated through some fun issues when I arrived, but I figured it out nonetheless. I had no data to make calls, so I relied on the Wi-Fi to call an Uber to go and pick up my angel girl. Luckily I prepared for this moment and had all the necessary information I needed on hand. I arrived at the facility and went back and forth to a few places in between trying to locate miss Tsuki. After a few hours of anxiety and the threat of additional fees, I managed to retrieve my little love.

To every small-minded person who told me, "Oh, the horror stories of transporting your pet?! The Horror! It's so dangerous."

Suck it.

The vet spoke English! I asked her to call an Uber for me because I didn't have any data, and there was no Wi-Fi available. She said, "I'm not allowed to do that," and speedily walked away from me. That good ol' nosebleed was starting to creep up on me again, but I managed to befriend the security guard there with my *very* limited Spanish, and out of the graciousness of his heart, he called a taxi for me. I was beyond grateful to just receive a little help when I needed it. Sometimes it is hard to ask for help, but doing so is the only way forward.

We made our trek to the Airbnb I would be staying at that week before making my way out to my friend. There was a small wait before the check-in, mainly because I was late and unable to communicate that with the hosts. They told me I would have to wait three hours, so I resigned myself to a bench with Miss Tsuki, turned on an audiobook, and just held my dog close. I was so grateful to just have this moment with her and to finally be here. It didn't even feel real that I was here.

Over and over, I was told by others that she's just a dog, and that I should go regardless of her. They didn't know the promise I made to her in Virginia, and I'm not the type of man to dishonor his vows. Despite the seemingly impossible requirements of getting her here, I succeeded. I could have given up after the first three tries, but I kept pushing because I refused to leave her behind. I'm not the only one who lost something; she lost things she cared about, too. Love isn't about convenience, it is about loyalty.

No longer was she able to sit and enjoy the ocean breeze on our balcony whenever she wanted. Home became a moving place to her; each time she got settled in again, I was back on the road. Her mom was no longer part of the picture, and KGB cat was no longer around for them to torment each other. Life was so different, and now she just endured a crazy flight with her dad, and all the dogs here speak a different language. It must have been quite confusing; however, I was determined to make it up to her with salmon with some sweet potato for dinner tonight and a long walk!

Fortunately, my waiting time was cut short as the receptionist came back early to let me in. I was grateful that a little patience freed me of stress and that the problem resolved itself.

Sometimes it feels like the world is just testing our mettle. They give us these little problems to see how we react to them. If we cannot summon the strength and grace to navigate small inconveniences, how will we have the strength to tackle bigger goals, like freedom?

I felt that I passed yet another test and made my way up to my apartment. I booked a penthouse suite for us for pennies in comparison to what it would have cost in the States. I placed my bags down and headed straight for the shower. The water pressure was immaculate, and the water was hot—*the good, perfect, wash-all-the-stress away kind of hot*. I tend to take inferno showers, then cool off at the end with an ice shower. After about 20 minutes in there, I felt all the grime and stress wash off me. I was tempted to roll into bed but knew that was not the move.

I only had a few hours before I was supposed to sign in for work, so I had to spend this time wisely. I took Tsuki on a nice walk through the city to help her stretch her legs and to see what was around me. I stopped at a pandería for some fresh hot bread, a San Marco pastry, and *una cerveza*.

I returned to the apartment with some time to spare and prepared myself to work. I ordered some groceries via Uber-Eats, which was extremely clutch, and some Monster Energy to help me power through the night.

I had about an hour to spare after all was said and done, so I listened to my body and took a quick nap on the couch.

When my alarm sounded, it felt as if I still needed another four hours of sleep, but this cog needed to turn. I rolled off of the couch and did some pushups to get my blood pumping. Then I sighed loudly, as I do when I'm stressed, and cracked open an energy drink.

I set up a little working spacing for myself, connected my HDMI cable to the TV as an extra monitor, and planted myself down for some agony. I ground through my workload for the day, determined to prove to everyone that I was capable of completing the work regardless of where I was.

I pushed through until about 2 a.m., and then closed my laptop with another big sigh and said, "Blood sacrifices."

I stepped outside on the terrace of the penthouse and took a minute to just look up at the sky and accept that I made it. It didn't feel real to me that I was here, but all the evidence pointed to the contrary. I wasn't quite as free as I wanted to be, but I was a dog with a little more leash, or more so a wolf caught in a trap—dare I chew my leg off to escape? I was not quite there yet, but I was going to figure it out.

I stared at the night sky, pulled the cold air into my lungs, and meditated in silence.

I'm coming for you, Levanter, I heard you, and I am here. Like my friend Kvothe from The Kingkiller Chronicles, *I am determined to know your name. Like Santiago from* The Alchemist, *I am determined to change the structure of my being and to become...wind.*

Shortly after, I crawled into bed, Tsuki cuddled into a ball next to my face, and we both rested.

I took some initiative over the next few days to get settled in and to buy a mobile data plan out here. Verizon wanted to charge me $10 a day for data, whereas you can simply get a data plan out here for $35 a month with a SIM card. It is a no-brainer. My confidence in my Spanish grew, as I had no other choice but to succeed. I had managed to claim Tsuki from freight forwarders, so getting my data plan was a breeze in the park. I even worked on my generally terrible sense of direction by getting to the mall to buy the SIM card. I was quite proud of myself! Slowly, I was tackling areas I was deficient in.

When I returned to the apartment, I had all I needed, except…a SIM card key for my phone.

After a LARGE sigh, I turned to good ol' logic: "When in lack, improvise." With not a single paper clip in sight, I ripped a staple off of one of my documents and opened the tray on my phone after 30 minutes of trying everything that didn't require me to leave again. When the tray snapped open, I heard the sound from *The Legend of Zelda* when Link opens a treasure chest. There is nothing like the reward of victory for a dedicated effort!

I also came to realize over the next few days that Tsuki's separation anxiety had gone down tremendously. I used to not be able to leave her behind to run simple errands without her thinking I was abandoning her. However, I think this flight, although it was stressful, instilled some trust in her that no matter how bad it gets, her dad will take care of her. I was relieved to see her relax a little more and just enjoy the breeze on the terrace like the old days.

When the weekend came, I was determined to explore, so I set out to the Prado Museum. The line to get inside was incredibly long, yet my love of museums and art, REAL ART—not a banana duct taped to a wall—overcame the dread of waiting in line. Once inside, I explored the vast museum top to bottom. Unfortunately, photography was not allowed, but I made it a point to just soak in the pieces that stood out to me. I haven't been an expert in art since that one semester in my freshman year of college, but I can appreciate a masterpiece when I see one.

I found myself being particularly drawn to the work of Peter Paul Rubens. I was captured by the imagery from his oil painting "Saint George and the Dragon." It was an image from the legend where Saint George slays a tyrannical dragon that terrorizes a town. It depicts Saint George clad in silvery armor on a white horse with a raised short sword to save the princess and the townspeople. The people would offer two sheep a day to appease the dragon, and when out of sheep, they used a lottery system for their children to be sent off. Only after converting to Christianity did Saint George slay the dragon. It was not quite as heroic as I would have liked; however, it was a completely fair negotiation in my opinion. I was staring at a painting that was over 400 years old, as this was the original work. What genius it takes to make something so incredible! It was something that millions of people have studied, admired, and gone to see over the centuries.

I was also drawn to the work of Miguel Ximinez in his depiction of "San Miguel," or Saint Michael the Arch Angel. This was *clearly* an attempt to show off how cool he thought his name was, but regardless, I was captivated. I was raised Catholic for a short period of time and was always fascinated with Saint Michael. He was God's strongest angel and battled demons and Lucifer, the father of lies himself, with his sword of holy fire, "The Flame of Death," that vanquishes all things demonic and evil. Only he could use the sword as the most powerful and loyal angel of God.

I always admired his strength, his justice, and his ability to defeat evil. The image portrayed a warlike angel clad in a red garb and red wings that had facets similar to a peacock's feathers. He bore a spear in his hand and slayed the demon before his feet with his righteous might. This painting was more than 500 years old, and I had the privilege of admiring it in person.

As I continued to wander about, I saw other works that I liked, such as Hercules and Namean Lion and the statue of Charles V and the Fury. I was shocked when I saw a painting of the Mona Lisa! I couldn't believe it was here—I thought it was supposed to be in France! However, I realized I was right, and that this version was done by one of Leonardo da Vinci's students. This didn't take anything away from the art to me; however, it made me understand the importance of originality. Although this work was undoubtedly just as good—if not better—than the original, no one knows this painter, yet everyone knows da Vinci.

After a few hours of soaking in everything I could absorb, I made my way to the gift shop and cafe. I bought some little souvenirs, including a bookmark of the Ximinez painting and magnets of the Mona Lisa and Saint George. As I walked to the cafe, it finally hit me: I've been here before! I completely forgot that I had been to this museum before and tried to remember as best as I could why, then I realized that it was because our class was in a rush, and we spent about 30 minutes there in total. I remember that I promised myself to return one day and to do it right because I hate being rushed when I'm trying to appreciate something. Seven years later, the scales have finally been balanced.

I sat down and had an amazing lunch inside of the museum. If I were a local, I would come all the time just for the ambiance and the food. If there is one thing the Spanish know how to do, it's carbs. They are loco for bocadillos and make some awesome cakes and coffee. I had this delicious ham and cheese sandwich on bread that was like a puff pastry with melted cheese on top. *Sinful.* I need you to understand that it wasn't simply cheese on top, but cheese that was infused within the bread itself. When they toasted the sandwich for me, it had that melted texture mixed with the remarkably fluffy bread. When I finished up my lunch, I indulged in a slice of carrot cake and a cafe con leche. It was remarkable to just sit in silence and enjoy a meal all by myself. I had not gone out to eat much over the last few months, but it had been oddly liberating going by myself. I like to sit in cafes and enjoy the company of a book and my notes as I just think about and entertain possibilities and schemes in my mind. On occasion, Tsuki tags along with me when it is permitted, but she isn't much of a conversationalist. She also likes to sit and stew in her philosophical contemplations.

After the museum, I still wasn't quite done exploring, so I decided to just roam around and enjoy the architecture of Madrid. I stumbled upon a botanical garden, took a brisk walk through there, and then walked through another park and serendipitously found the Palacio de Cristal. I wasn't expecting to find that in the park, but nevertheless, I just let the sense of wonder wash over me.

My walk slowly came to an end, and I was exhausted, having walked more than 18 miles that day in pure exploration. I felt some hunger come over me, and a headache crept in that I tried to ignore. I picked up some wine and more groceries for dinner and laughed as a cart full of groceries only cost 20 Euros here versus about double in the States.

I tried to unwind when I returned to the apartment and planned for the next day. I had booked a surprise for my friend and me to go horseback riding in the mountains tomorrow. Unfortunately, he had to cancel at the last minute, but I was still committed to going. I woke up with a minor migraine in the morning and knew that it was about to be a difficult day since I wasn't able to sleep it off, but alas, I kept pressing forward.

I took an Uber out of Madrid and towards the town of Navacerrada, where I met an interesting man named Mariano. He was a humble but proud man, content with the choices he made in life. I met him outside the gate of his property, and he picked me up in his pickup truck.

We chatted together as we went to pick up the other riders, and he started telling me about the mountains. He told me that these are the mountains that inspired Ernest Hemmingway to write *For Whom the Bell Tolls*. This made me laugh because the reference came seemingly out of nowhere, and he was surprised to learn that I had already read that book. I also spoke of *The Alchemist* and thought of the Levanter passing through the mountains.

I asked him, "How long have you been doing these tours?"

He told me, "For the past 25 years, I've lived on my land, on *my* mountain. I used to work in business, but it was killing me. I woke up one day and realized I was not happy with my life, and each day I woke up to work it made me sad, and I felt like life wasn't worth living. One day, I decided to just quit and move to the mountain. It was property in my family, but now it is my land. I'm not a very rich man, but I am happy. I love living out here with my dogs and horses and hunting with my eagle."

Hunting with an eagle? That is about the most metal thing I have ever heard, 10/10 will have to try it one day.

The sentiment was all too familiar to me, and I was happy that one man found his freedom. I shared that I also work in business and understood what he meant. I told him it was admirable for him to follow his true love.

The love of life should always matter more than the love of money; however, due to inflation, the freedom to love life has become more expensive. I also didn't have any relatives with horse ranches to give to me—at least, none that I knew of. If so, please feel free to reach out, let's get a drink and ride some horses.

We slowly gathered the other passengers, and to my surprise, they are all relatively close to my age and all from different countries. We had a couple from Brazil, and in another couple, one was from France and the other from the United Kingdom. The second relationship made me laugh, a true Romeo and Juliet centuries later. From bitter enemies to a loving couple, my, how the times have changed. Then there was me, just me.

I found myself feeling a little lonely in the face of these couples and wished that I had someone with me, too. Some days, I still can't believe that my marriage is over; it's similar to the feeling of letting go of a balloon. You let go, but you still can't believe it's gone. I would have loved to share this experience with her, but the truth is, the only reason I can experience this is because she is gone. It's a hard truth to swallow, yet 'tis the cost of freedom, I suppose.

I've never ridden a horse before, but I've known some cowgirls in my time, ayeeeee. Kidding. Maybe. Inappropriate? I don't care.

I approached my noble steed. He was a white horse with some freckled spots—not exactly a Ryushadium from Roshar or a Kershean from Temerant, but he was my stallion. I asked Mariano what his name was because, if you know, *all names have power in them*. He told me his name was "Garavasto." I followed up and asked what the meaning of his name was, and he said, "Nothing! Just some random sounds."

I thought that was funny, so to me, Garavasto meant "serendipity." There I was, riding Serendipity in the mountains, with curiosity by my side and beauty before my eyes. I did a pretty good job riding my first time. Garavasto was a sneaky horse. He knew the trail well, so he took shortcuts whenever he could or would simply stop walking because he knew the group was going to turn around. I understood his mindset and found it to be charming and mischievous.

Mariano took us along *his* mountainside, and we saw the Seven Peak Mountains in the distance. I knew that Segovia waited on the other side of it. I visited Segovia on my last trip to Spain, and the architecture was stunning, especially the large aqueduct that bisected the town. The town was known for crispy suckling pig, and from what I remember, it was perfectly salty and crunchy. Perhaps I'll be able to find some later.

We quickly breezed through the mountains and enjoyed the fresh air and the sights around us. When we approached the end of the trail, Garavasto suddenly found a new wind and galloped a little to the finish line.

You witty horse, you are just sprinting towards your break.

We all said our thanks to Mariano, and he drove us to the bus stop in his truck. This time I decided to sit in the bed of the truck so I could enjoy the breeze and get some photos as I left. It was a little bumpy, but I was starting to feel it, that sensation of freedom I was looking for.

I laughed to myself, took some jamón out of my bag, and started snacking away.

Ah, Garavasto, thank you for carrying me through the mountainside. You were a wonderful horse, and I hope you get some rest today. I feel what Robert Jordan from Hemmingway's novel felt: "fully integrated."

When we arrived at the bus stop, I mentioned that I was just going to walk toward town. Mariano was kind enough to offer me a ride instead—he just asked that I write about him in my book.

Well, I kept my promise, friend. Thanks again.

I was stunned by the beauty of the town of Navacerrada. The streets were lively with people, but in a warm and welcoming kind of way. Everyone was sitting outside and enjoying a meal with friends and family. The mountains loomed over the horizon, and it was a perfect view of beauty.

As I walked through the city, there were two young boys throwing stones into the street as they sat on a ledge by a park. I tried to walk around them when one of them stopped me. "Tengo una pregunta," he said. I paused, a little nervous that if they didn't like my answer, they would throw some stones at me. "De dónde eres?" he said.

I laughed to myself and thought, "Well, that's not good. Apparently, I stick out so obviously that even children can tell that I'm not from here."

I later came to realize that my baseball cap was a dead giveaway that I was an American.

"Vale, cuál es tu pregunta?" I said.

"Que ciudad vives?" he asked.

"He vivido en muchas ciudades de Estados Unidos, pero soy de Nueva York," I said.

He responded with something that I couldn't understand but then said in English, "New York, it is very beautiful!"

I had to keep myself from laughing out loud. These children lived in a beautiful, quiet mountainside town where there was just so much life happening. They lived in an actual oasis of beauty and warmth, and they called New York "beautiful."

I responded, "No, esta ciudad es hermosa! Pero, yo entiendo. Una día, tienes que viajar a Nueva York! Algo mas?"

"No, gracias," he said.

I walked away after a friendly "adios." I was relieved they decided not to throw rocks, but I was starving and needed something to eat. My migraine had gotten significantly worse, and I was growing nauseous. I went into a restaurant and requested a table for one. The waitress questioned me when I said, "Solomente me," but then seated me.

I laughed to myself, "Was that pity?"

Ah, to some, being alone seems sad or scary, and they aren't completely wrong. However, sometimes being alone is beautiful and gives us some time to figure ourselves out. I wish I could have shared it with her, but I reminded myself that the past is the past. I had been talking to someone new for a while, too, and I know she would have wanted to be here. That also could have been nice. There are people out there, Ethan, who are willing to love you, but you, you are not ready to love someone else yet. Are you?

After a quiet sigh to myself, I answered my own question.

No, I'm not ready. I wish I were. Being in love is a beautiful thing, but I'm just not ready to trust another woman yet. How do I know they will honor their commitments? How do I know they mean what they say? I don't, and it's also my fault because I'm not ready to give someone the chance to prove me wrong. The thing is, I'm rarely wrong about people, and that's why this one hurts so much. I was so wrong, so, so wrong. I thought we built something lasting together. I thought it mattered, but I was wrong.

What was the change? How does "I love you" turn into "I hate you"? When does that happen, exactly? Why did it happen? So be it. In the words of this new almost-love of mine, "Very well." I'm sorry I couldn't give you the chance; my heart was just too broken, and I didn't want to break yours, too.

I enjoyed a solemn and delightful meal. The moment was shared only with my thoughts, and then head back to the apartment. My true love greeted me at the door. I know she will only break my heart once, but she doesn't know that and never will.

My migraine was only getting worse, and I started to break down a little. The room was spinning, and the lights were blinding—not to mention, the pungent smell of my Uber driver's cologne almost set me over the edge. Spanish men like to peacock with their colognes and often wear A LOT of it, and when I get migraines, my sense of smell and light sensitivity go through the roof. I have a sharp sense of smell in general, but wow, was it bad when I was in this state. I gritted my teeth and held my breath at times to avoid throwing up. I started to plan my train ticket for the next day and realized that my dog crate was too big for the Renfe, and that I needed something else. I rushed out to two pet stores, desperately trying to get a crate so that I could rest tonight before my departure to El Puerto de Santa Maria. The first store didn't have what I needed, so I rushed to yet another store, and the Uber driver dropped me off about half a mile off point with only 10 minutes to spare before the store closed.

I stood there in the night, head pounding, weighing my odds. Then, I just started running, I kept a medium pace and was surprised that I was just gliding through, and it didn't seem so hopeless. I made it to the store with two minutes to spare, grabbed my crate, and was all set for tomorrow.

I took one ride home, and the pungent cologne of my driver nearly killed me on top of running with a migraine, but I survived.

I just need rest, I just need rest. Hold out a little more.

When I got back inside, I dropped into my bed and slept for several hours. When I woke up, I still felt weak and needed to do something.

It was midnight, and I dragged myself out of bed to get dressed. I was too dizzy to take an Uber, especially with the high likelihood they would be wearing strong cologne. I decided to walk over to a pharmacy. To my surprise, there was a long line outside at midnight. Then, a little girl from hell, about 12 years old but apparently severely coddled by her mother, just ran about making noise, rattling chains on the shopping carts, and breaking out into song. I considered walking into to traffic to stop the headache, but I persisted.

When it was nearly my turn in line, the two of them cut right to the front because they would only need a "quick thing." I chuckled bitterly to myself, "Ah, I see where she gets it from." Eventually, I got my pain medicine and felt much better. I realized that I over-exerted myself the previous day by walking 18 miles and not eating enough protein and carbs to sustain me. I realized that I had dropped into ketosis and was experiencing a migraine from eating an insufficient amount of fat. It turns out one cannot sustain themselves on bocadillos and croquettas.

At about 1 a.m., I crawled back inside, victorious but exhausted. I took some paracetamol and knocked out.

The next morning, I felt much better. I was able to remedy the situation the next day with some "bulletproof" coffee. It's basically just a big dollop of grass-fed butter in coffee with some sugar. The fat would help meet my macro quota to help alleviate my headache. If only broken hearts were as easy to fix as headaches. I gathered my belongings, took Tsuki on a long walk, and did a sweep of the apartment to make sure I had everything.

"Good to go!"

Yet another flight for the Lastavica to take—or rather, a train ride. The only problem is that freedom is never a train ride or flight away. Freedom is love. I feel free when I have love in my heart. I can't rely on her any longer to give me that, so I have to start loving myself a little, as cheesy as it sounds. I have to create that sense of freedom within myself. I can't keep sprinting off in one direction or another looking for it; it has been, and always will be, a feeling inside of me.

I decide if I'm chained or free. My mind holds the shackles despite the cries of my heart. I think I'm starting to understand what that means.

Chapter 9

THE CALL OF THE LEVANTER

March 10, 2023

I arrived at Mardrid Anotocha Estacion de Tren and trudged on with all my luggage. Once again, I recalled that I had been here before. What struck me most about this station was its unique blend of architectural beauty and nature. The inner atrium, adorned with lush greenery, seemed to reflect Spain's appreciation for the natural world as an art form.

I wasn't really in the mood to stop and take pictures, as I was stressed waiting for the train—or, moreso, eager to reach my destination. My buddy was supposed to come out to help me transfer over, but something came up at the last second, and I had to cut some freight weight. I abandoned Tsuki's travel crate, and a single tear escaped as I saw $135 poof into smoke in front of me. My hands were full with my suitcase in tow, backpack fully loaded, and angel-winged doggo in her carrier. I navigated toward my track, a half man, half machine, half pack-mule beast, trudging along. I laughed to myself as I acknowledged that this year was about letting go of the past. I'm frequently put in positions where I have no other choice but to simply let go. Maybe that's my lesson.

I was expecting the train station to feel more like Penn Station in NY, but it was closer to an experience at the airport. I even had to go through a security checkpoint with Tsuki before getting through the gate. Unfortunately, my train was about an hour and a half late—which, I have come to realize, is rather unusual for the Renfe. They take quite a bit of pride in running efficiently and being on time. This worked out tremendously in my favor because they ended up refunding all the passengers 50% of their ticket, and it was a 134 Euro ticket, so that was pretty cool. Yet again, patience was rewarded.

I feel like I have always been in a rush, sprinting towards my goals. I never stop or even try to slow down to smell the roses. I have been trying to get better at appreciating the small moments in life. It's hard to be present when you are always thinking you can't be happy until some future date...

Unlike Penn Station, when the track was announced, everyone proceeded in an orderly fashion and got in the queue to scan their tickets. In Penn Station, when the second the track is announced, bedlam explodes, and all the corporate folk sprint towards their tracks to return to Long Island. We are like rats in a maze at Penn: eagerly, we stare at the track board, ticking with irritation, impatiently waiting for the dopamine hit of seeing TRACK 17, TRACK 18, or TRACK 19. We sprint to the track because it is the opportunity for us to finally rest. We are so desperate to get back home to just try and secure five whole minutes to ourselves...

I hauled my luggage into the designated luggage areas, threw my backpack on an overhead rack, and took my seat with Tsuki on my lap. I came to admire the cleanliness and efficiency of their system. Unlike the Long Island Railroad in New York, which is just a mindless free-for-all, the Renfe had some order. Remarkably, there was no trash on the floor or people peeing in the carts, and there were assigned seats! It was a true sight of beauty for a planner such as myself who seeks order in a chaotic world. It was so calm that it almost made me feel uneasy. I was certainly far from home.

It was about a five-hour train ride to El Puerto de Santa Maria, but I was not dreading it. My train rides to and from Madrid were honestly some of the highlights of this trip for me. Truly, if you are from an urban environment me like me, it is such an amazing contrast. The train glides on a track through the mountainside. The sky is painted blue, and large jet streams and clouds fill the blank space. We would pass the quiet homes of farmers or shepherds and see herds of sheep and horses. At one station, there was an older man with a cane with a palm full of bird seeds. Vibrant green birds perched on his wrists, and everyone smiled in admiration of this man. Although I was inside the train cart, I could imagine the feeling of the wind brushing through my hair and what it would be like to just fly over the countryside, free and uninhibited.

If I were a local in Spain, I would take a train ride like this once a week so I could enjoy this space to think, read, and write in private. I pulled out my copy of *The Island of the World* to read a little more about the adventure of Josip Lasta, but after a few pages in, tears started to well in my eyes. Josip is just a soul of the world, a person who has lived so much life in such a short time. He frequently loses everything sacred to him, stripped of his family, his name, his clothes, and his dignity; yet despite his struggles, he just can't allow himself to give up. He pulls strength from the well of his soul to simply survive and find the right way to walk through the world. His wounds scar around his heart, and a smile becomes the callous he wears on his face. His intimate experiences with depravity and devastation only make him pull more humanity from the well of strength beyond his despair. Often those who feel spited by the world will inflict further wounds on others to create a sort of Karmic balance. Those people drag others down to their state of emotional understanding to help justify their anger or inaction. However, some feel the pain so deeply that they never wish to inflict it on others. By sitting with their thoughts, they introspect and face their demons so that they can help others face theirs, too. He was young, but his eyes were filled with wisdom, an understanding of the world, and the true hearts of men and women.

In the scene I was reading, he was with a family he met along the way of his travels. He saw the beautiful love a father has for his children. The sacrifices a father makes without ever asking for a single thanks likely reminded him of his own father. The man's children would always say that their father hates chocolate because he always gives his pieces to them and their mom. The man's name is Emilio, and he is a dentist; he would sacrifice all of his wealth to serve his community. As a dentist, he frequently took patients that came with more cost than gain because it was the right thing to do. He lived humbly with a simple car and a simple home because the luxury in the face of his duty would have felt shameful to him. Emilio had helped Josip "get his smile back" after he lost most of his teeth from a beating he endured when imprisoned.

Josip saw the true heart of Emilio, and as a thank you, he made a gift for Emilio and his wife, Slavica. To Slavica, he gave a poem:

> *"In a father's toil-worn face can be read the epic tale:*
> *Within his eyes is a boy I once knew*
> *Though we never met*
> *See how he carries you and carries me*
> *And the offspring of his soul*
> *As if we weigh no more than birds perching on his fingertips*
> *Yet are dearer to him than the stars*
>
> *It is there in his eyes, not easily read,*
> *Each tried man is like this, holding within himself*
> *A world that once was, a world that may be made anew*
> *He knows himself as incomplete, sees the failures*
> *As do all men before the ending of their tale.*
> *Though with each ending a beginning is writ,*
> *Each death is a birth for which he knows full well the cost*
> *Yet this price could not be paid alone, without you."*

To Emilio, he gave a bar of Swiss chocolate. It was a gesture that moved him deeply and confused his children. Chocolate was quite the rarity for the time and, as such, was expensive. Emilio sat in stunned silence looking at his gift while his children exclaimed that he may have mixed up the gifts! Their

Papa never ate chocolate, but their mom did, and to them, the poem was clearly about their Papa!

Oftentimes, children don't understand or appreciate the unwavering love a parent has for them—that is, until they become parents themselves. There is an instinct to simply "go without" in the face of making sure their child does not starve for something they want. How I understood the poem was that Emilio, and all fathers, will sacrifice and endure if it means providing for their family. They will fight their own silent battles while projecting strength for their families, so it is important that Slavica truly sees the man underneath the masks of "father" and "husband." Josip was trying to show her that he makes all those sacrifices out of love, and that he wouldn't be able to do any of it without her. As for Emilio, the chocolate was an acknowledgment of his sacrifices, a token of admiration for seeing the truth of his character, and a reminder that even he has to stop to enjoy life's sweetness once in a while; otherwise, the whole world seems bitter.

To spare myself the embarrassment of crying in public, I decided to pick this up again later.

I like to savor this book when I have a moment for quiet reflection, but alas, I decided to pick up a different title on my Audible account, *Psycho-Cybernetics* by Maxwell Maltz with Matt Fury's commentary. This book is about being a cyborg psychopath and the augmentation of human performance through digital integration.

Kidding.

It is a fascinating read in the personal development space that is not just another lame "seven rules, 92 laws, 15 gameplans" or some other understimulating book, like *Who Moved My Cheese* or *The Secret*. If you want to learn something rather than be vaguely "motivated" for a couple of days, only to forget all the lessons later, read this book. The quintessential ethos of the book is to help the reader adjust their perception of self and to understand why they have that perception to begin with. In his commentary, he finds that people often associate an emotional value with an event that may not be factually true. This emotional value can impair someone's self-perception and their ability to perform. One example in the book was an entrepreneur who lost about $200,000 in the stock market. He started associating this event emotionally as "I am a failure. I am an idiot." His confidence eroded, he became consumed with that loss, and it eroded his trust in his own decisions for fear of repeating the same failure. However, although he did fail and lose that money, that does not mean that he was a failure. He became absorbed by the gravity of his loss to the point where it consumed his identity.

I think it is in human nature to spend more time identifying with the worst moments in our lives rather than the best. I'm not different from anyone else; I feel that tinge of shame or disappointment from those moments I wish just didn't happen. I have failed so many times at some many things, especially the things I really care about. However, failure is just part of the process. I have recently decided to stop calling failed attempts failures, and instead, I say, "I am learning, or still learning." It's a simple shift in perspective that affords me some grace. I hate to tell you, but all talent to the side, everyone sucks when they first start something. There is always room for refinement, but we halt our progress the moment we impose the title of failure on ourselves.

The chapter that stood out the most to me was chapter 11, "Unlocking Your Real Personality." The chapter spoke to the concept of "inhibition." Essentially, based on how we are raised, we develop certain levels of inhibition as conditioned by our environments. For example, I have always been more of an introvert, and it is because of how my social interactions would go. At home, I would frequently hear the aphorism, "Children are meant to be seen and not heard." This taught me to be silent, because if I spoke, it was inappropriate or embarrassing to my parents. I also frequently changed schools when I was younger because my family moved quite a bit, and being the "new kid" makes you an outcast. It would tend to come with the challenges of being a young boy around other young boys who are all trying to understand where they stand in their social hierarchies. I learned to stay to myself because new interactions in school led to fights, and speaking at home led to swift punishment. I learned that I had nothing of value to offer people and to stay silent and incognito. I didn't want to draw unwanted attention to myself from aggressive people in my environment.

I developed a level of inhibition that encouraged me to retreat within myself. I felt that there wasn't a place for me in the world, and that I never quite measured up to the expectations of others. I developed social inhibition but countered that reaction with a strong internal drive for success. I felt that people treated me like I was stupid, and that I was harshly punished for failure. This isn't something imagined up from a child's understanding of the world, but I was called every name under the sun by both bullies and family that also fell into that category. I was rarely ever just "Ethan," but I was called "retard," "moron," "jackass," and more. Hearing these untruths caused a great deal of turmoil for me because I rejected their views of me. It pushed me to work harder. I wanted to show those people that I was smart, capable, and kind. I wanted the results that I produced to be undeniable so that no one could call me stupid anymore.

I strive for excellence in anything I do because I am curious about what I am capable of, but also because of that chip that still sits on my shoulder. I still have that piece of me that says, "Watch me, bitch." Watch me smash your expectations, watch me set the bar and succeed no matter what. You can't break me, you don't know me, you don't know what I am capable of. I've always worked hardest when I felt I had something to prove. I was able to produce results, straight A's, Advance Placement classes, and moving weight in the gym. I cared about being optimal; however, the problem became not that I couldn't prove it to "them," but that I could not prove it to myself that I was capable.

I'd still hear the naysayers in my head telling me I'm not good enough, but their voices became my voice. I was never satisfied with anything I did. I just didn't get that dopamine drip of accomplishment, but instead saw 10 other ways I could be better. I was cursed by the pursuit of perfection.

I realized that now is the time to grow out of this narrative, and those relationships, if need be. I needed to stop suppressing myself and my desire to be someone who can create value. It was honestly interesting taking on this new mindset because it also tested who was truly my friend and who truly accepted me. It led to some really funny moments for me down the road when I would discuss these ideas and changes in personality with the "Crew."

It was quite amusing when Desire posed the following question to the group: "Who would win in a fight?" Typically, I'd avoid such inquiries to sidestep any appearance of arrogance, but this time, the answer seemed glaringly obvious. It meant delving into thoughts best left unspoken to avoid straining friendships.

Desire then narrowed it down, suggesting it would be either Lag or me who stood out in the group. Once again, the impulse to speak truthfully was overshadowed by social expectations. Despite the discomfort, I pushed myself out of my comfort zone and proclaimed, "I would win." I then explained to my friends that such candor was uncharacteristic of me.

A minor protest ensued, as fighting often stirs the male ego. Hypothetical scenarios were thrown my way in an attempt to undermine my assertion. However, I found these arguments flimsy and amusing. Despite the unease it caused, I felt compelled to express my genuine beliefs rather than be disingenuous. I confidently stated, "Without a doubt, I would emerge victorious every single time."

Perhaps it was an overcompensation for my usual introversion, but everyone has to start somewhere. After all, they are my friends, and they understand my sense of humor.

Some argued, "If they did x, y, z, they would win." However, I emphasized that I never stopped training, and my skills surpassed theirs, especially in striking. I made it clear that additional training was unnecessary; if a confrontation were to happen here and now, I would prevail.

Concluding the debate in a light-hearted manner, I remarked, "It's refreshing to speak my mind without fearing consequences."

Ultimately, if I can't be honest with my brothers, then who can I be honest with? It's been months since that conversation, and no one has embarked on hypothetical training except for Desire, who occasionally boxes now.

I was constantly suppressing myself to fit in the box of the expectations of others. People said I am arrogant for writing a book, I'm "douchey" for having muscles, and I am a "wantraprenuer."

It appears, that every time that I tried to be more than what I was, I was being arrogant, so why even try? Despite, the general lack of support, I still see what I want for myself in the future. Except now, one thing has changed: I am no longer suppressing that version of myself that sees my potential. I no longer feel the need to make myself meek and small to feel the acceptance of others.

It's an odd trend in my generation to embrace "body positivity," except that doesn't seem to apply to those who work hard to achieve physiques, improve their health, or compete. Body positivity seems to only be for people who are lazy and want to justify their inaction with false praise and false acceptance. Everyone wants to be accepted, but why must we stoop to delusions to find it—and, worse than that, let others feed the delusions? Truth and reality seem to fall further and further away under the false guise of love and acceptance. It feels like the Devil's work, a poisonous group think that corrupts truth and lowers our consciousness by the right of sanctimony.

You have no idea how irritating I find it when people feel they have a free pass to comment on my appearance. "Oh, are you on a tren, bro?"
"Wow, you must have great genetics man!"
"Some people just can't achieve that, you know, it's not realistic."
"You look like such a douche right now…"

Nope, genetics has nothing to do with it.

People **LOVE** to find excuses to justify why others can do something and they can't. It is so much easier to believe that they were born with some kind of limitation that cheated them out of ever being better than they are. I always found it so irritating how many won't even consider the possibility of something before writing it off as impossible. I find it to be a cowardly way to live. I have to realize that when I hear those voices, they are just coming from a place of insecurity in others. They just assume that I magically woke up fit, and that I'm lucky; however, what they don't see is that young teenager walking into the weight room in freshman year of high school. They don't see the boy who wants to be strong so that he can defend his family and himself from evil. I often felt powerless as a child, and as such, I could not adequately defend myself or those whom I cared about. My mind has never truly known a time of peace; it was always moving from one struggle to another. The only two options were to endure or surrender. There was just so much frustration, sadness, and ambition wrapped up inside of me that I focused it all into personal development. I felt so alone, and I realized that if I was going to be alone, I needed the strength—both mentally and physically—to carry that burden.

I was pulled out of my book and reflection when the man across from me became inspired to have a conversation with me.

Yet another test.

Stepping out of my comfort zone, I engaged. He was an older man. He was portly with a gray beard and was wearing a Spanish fodera.

I was tempted to get one several times but never pulled the trigger.

As it was still my first week in Spain, my Spanish was still pretty rough around the edges. I fumbled my way through the conversation, and we exchanged niceties about where we were from, information about my dog, and some general likes and dislikes. I would get nervous when I didn't know the words to describe something, but my new friend Victor was very kind and patient. He would just say, "Tranquilo," when I stumbled. The use of the word "tranquilo" always carried a gravitas to me. It translates to "be tranquil." Nervousness is so foreign to the Spanish that it appears chaotic for someone to be mildly anxious for not finding a word.

Despite my limited Spanish, we somehow managed to speak for about an hour. I appreciated his gregariousness and accepted that I could afford to lower my guard in Spain a little. It is hard to explain, but in New York, the general sense of aggression around me was always hovering around a seven to an eight. People are pretty strung out back home, enraged by traffic, wages that never seem to be enough in the face of increasing prices, and our default "stay the fuck out of my way" energy. The contrast was hilarious; in Spain, everyone is so relaxed, and I think it is because they live more fulfilling lives. They don't care about buying a $40,000 car and aren't big on "hustle" culture. They just eat outside a lot with friends and family, walk everywhere, and enjoy fresh food, hot bread, and sweet wine. They also take a lot of pride in their city and keep it clean, and they go as far as washing the streets at night. What I have later come to learn is that nine out of ten times when you speak with a local, they don't really care that you don't speak perfectly as long as you share a little bit of why you love it in their country.

Eventually, the conversation ran dry, and I was left with my thoughts again. I was once five hours away from my destination, but now it was five minutes. "What are the odds?" I thought to myself. First, there was Kerri, whom I met in the fifth grade and who gave me a haven when I needed one, and now it is Jeff, whom I also met in that grade. It is amazing how meeting new people can change your life in some of the most unexpected ways and at the most unexpected times.

Jeff has always been more like a brother to me rather than a friend. When we were young, we connected on an intellectual level. He was my first friend who I felt could keep up with my ambition and drive for success. We were always at the top of our class, and that gave us special privileges. I still remember that we were trusted to read *My Side of the Mountain* in a room separated from the rest of the class...and with no supervision.

We honestly read the entire book in a week and then spent the remaining two months just goofing around. One time, Jeff found a bunch of Domino's sugar packets into the storage closet and started going nuts like the Wolf of Wall Street—just a couple of ten-year-olds pretending to do lines of cocaine with sugar packets, playing Yu-Gi-Oh, and talking about how easy school is. We would also play chess when we had downtime, and he would always toss the board when I would win, a habit he did not grow out of! Although we don't see each other in person as often as we used to when we were young, we have managed to stay in touch by playing *Call of Duty* together. Amazingly, we have been playing the same game together for about 10 years now! The Covid pandemic was truly a golden age of gaming for us and all our old friends. It was amazing to see some of those old names signing online again to jump into the war zone for a battle royale. At one point, we were in the top one percent of all players, and we would celebrate hitting 50- and 100-win milestones with a drink and play day. *Good, simple times.*

My train rolled to a halt, and I gathered my belongings and made my way to my friend. I saw him in his Audi convertible, and he was wearing his black Dior jacket and Rayban aviators and had a fresh taper haircut. I laughed to myself, amused, and rolled my eyes while thinking, "This fucking guy is always so flashy!" He dapped me up, gave me a hug, and just like that, five years of not seeing each other in person just faded away. True friendships pick right back up where you left them.

"I can't believe you are here!" he said to me.

"Bro, I know, I can't believe I'm here either, man. Thanks for hosting me, I really appreciate it. It has been a tough time for me, man, and I am just trying to get my head on straight."

"I understand that. I know that you love Spain, so I thought this would be good for you, and I could use the company. Are you hungry? Let's go for drinks," he said.

Little did I know that this would be the beginning of him testing the outer limits of my liver for the next couple of months. Foolishly, I agreed, thinking that we would just get some tapas and a beer. Boy, I was wrong.

I got Tsuki settled in the house and in my room for now. It felt good to be a little settled again. I knew it was temporary, but staying in place for three months felt foreign to me because I have been on the move, hopping from Airbnb to Airbnb. On the outside, my friends would remark how exciting it was to be traveling, and they were half right. It was fun traveling and seeing new things, but the nights were rough. Most of the time, I felt like I was wrestling with my mind. I just kept trying to piece myself back together but was struggling to pick the pieces up. Right when I gathered a few shards in my hand, the earth would shake from, I don't know, a Suburban hitting me, or work pushing to put in 12–16 hours days. There was just an immense pressure to keep going no matter what, and I couldn't let myself stop. I couldn't let myself fall.

Putting my bags down, seeing fresh sheets on the bed, and having my dog safe and sound in Spain with me after several failed attempts caused a wave of relief to pass through my body. It has been pointed out to me that I often sigh, but it isn't from frustration necessarily. It's moreso a release of pressure building up inside of me.

Jeff handed me my own set of keys and said, "This your home, use it as such." I was deeply grateful for the compassion and bought the first round of drinks, and I became fluent in ordering gin and tonics over the next few months. We ended up drinking quite a bit, and he acted as the devil on my shoulder, putting more glasses in front of me as one emptied.

By the end of the night, we were stumbling home by 4 a.m. He proceeded to the kitchen, determined to make chicken "nuggies," and I retired to my room because I was working the next day.

I woke up with a super fun headache, but I was honestly a little relieved. I realized this was the first time I had hung out with a friend since all this madness started. It made me realize that "life is better with friends nearby." My ex was my "person," so losing her was more than just losing my wife, but also my best friend. I used to think that as long as we had each other, there would be no loneliness, but that proved to be an equation that didn't tie out.

"C'est la vie."

Tsuki honestly kept me all together this whole time, but I needed some humanity to rejuvenate my spirit.

Work was growing increasingly more frustrating because one of my coworkers and I were butting heads. He was extremely annoying and pessimistic, and he would remark, "I hope you can keep up with all your responsibilities in Spain." I sensed what he was implying and assured him that I would not have an issue doing my work, regardless of where I was. Our relationship got increasingly worse despite my efforts to pacify his micromanaging. Nothing irritates me more than stupidity, especially when someone I do not respect talks down to me.

I worked on complicated entries that had an excess of 50 tabs in an Excel file, and he would complain if a screenshot I took wasn't aligned in the sheet to his standard. He actually once marked up 25 comments on one of my workbooks because I didn't drag a formula down to sum up cells that had no value. Can you imagine that?! Twenty-five comments, all for the same thing of not summing a cell that did not even have a value of "0" in it. This was marked as an error, although it had no bearing on the outcome. People that act like this give me the feeling of "worms." It makes me cringe at how underhanded, petty, and irritating they can be. Unfortunately, he was like this with everything. God forbid I had a space when using a hyphen or used the wrong font; the poor man may have passed out and died.

Jeff would often sympathize, gloat, and remark, "Damn, dude, I thought you would be freer, but you work more than me, and I am in the military!" I would be anchored to my desk all day and was too anxious to step away for an hour so that I could explore Spain, but I eventually broke that mindset. Team members were dropping like flies, and the mountain of work grew ever taller. In a way, I was searching for the feeling I had from the first time I went to Spain in college, but there was just this giant emotional wall in front of me. I remember so vividly what it was like living León that summer, studying at the University there. I remember just enjoying the simple pleasures of walking through the city in the morning to get to the campus and the pleasure of having "un cafe con leche y un bocadillo de jamon y queso" for two Euros with my friends. We would all breeze through classes there; for once, I decided to do poorly on a skill level test there so I would get the easier Spanish classes.

The trip with my college cost about $5,000, and I remember talking to a rich girl who had gone the year before. I asked her how much pocket money I should bring, and she said another $5k. I rationalized that if the rich girl needed $5k,

I could probably be fine with two. I worked like a madman for months, picking up overtime shifts with my accounting "internship" with Estée Lauder. I was also actively investing a portion of my paycheck each week into stocks and ETFs as an accelerated savings plan for the trip. After months of laborious sacrifice and planning, I had not only paid for my trip by myself, but saved about $2,500 for me to enjoy myself while I was there.

It was the best time of my life, and it was the first time I truly felt free. I felt that when I walked the city, I was free of all ties and attachments. While Spain slept with their siestas—a marvelous idea—I would roam, read, and ruminate. I relished the fact that I did it myself; I got here by myself. The previous year, I wasn't able to go on a trip to Germany with my college cohort, and it crushed my spirit, so I decided that this year would be different with proper preparation. It felt surreal, and up until the moment I got on the plane, I was half expecting something to go wrong and take this opportunity from me. It was a taste of serendipity that I was even in Spain because I was planning on going to Belgium for a business competition. I had applied for a contest that my school hosted and wrote an essay on macro trends; however, I later came to find out that I was rejected due to a personal issue. I was shocked when I saw the docket of who was accepted for the trip and had a meeting with the advisors so that I could better prepare to participate in the next year. The conclusion wasn't that my submission was inferior, but that "two students were given 'Golden Willy Wonka tickets,' because they weren't able to go last year." I was told that I wasn't a "team player," despite building the largest business club on campus and hosting the largest collaborative event done to date at the college. It was all personal and favoritism. Meritocracy is all but dead; it's all about who you know and whose ass you kiss in corporate.

However, I have come to realize that all things happen for a reason. That trip was ultimately canceled due to global travel concerns—or in my mind, divine Karma. If I was selected to go, I would have missed the registration period for Spain and would have been home in NY for the summer. I'm glad that it all worked out for the best, and maybe there is some sort of cosmic hand guiding us to where we need to be...

Going to Spain was the first fruit of my labor to ever ripen. It's hard to explain, but I feel like I've always just been waiting for the other foot to fall when I experience something good. It was always a thought of, "Now, wait and watch as something ruins this." Perhaps it was a self-fulfilling prophecy to a degree, but *then again, a monk once gave me a fortune that my first 27 years of my life were supposed to be very unlucky. I didn't want to believe him, but...I digress. Actually boarding my plane and magically not being struck by lightning on my flight perplexed me when I landed. Magically, it all somehow worked out, and the best month of my life was about to begin.*

Recounting some of my sweetest memories of Spain inspired me to think about my old book, or rather the first book I wrote, *The Ink of My Soul and the Fire in My Bones*. It made me think of what that version of myself would say to me now. I winced at the thought of it, and in some ways I feel like I let him down. I dreamt of this time of my life so many times and envisioned what it would be like. I thought things would be different...but it is what it is.

I'd always dream of that future place where home would feel like a warm place to rest. I didn't have to worry about money, because I had an abundance of it and could take care of everyone. I owned my time and my freedom with the business I was buildin, so that I could explore all of my creative interests to my leisure.

However, I know that version of myself would prefer I didn't spiral in self-pity. I hope that part continues to haunt the cynic in me as I grow older. Life always has a purpose, but sometimes it is hard to see through our pain.

To honor my younger self and the man I strive to become, I decided it was a matter of principle that I savored this time to reflect and to enjoy where I was in the world. I loosened the binds of my imprisonment and slipped out the front door.

I am free. I am changing. I am becoming what I think about.

Chapter 10

THE CALLING OF SEEDS

March 28, 2023

I leashed the angel girl, grabbed a light jacket and sunglasses, and began to roam and ruminate with Miss Tsuki.

It felt slightly off from what I envisioned Spain to feel like, partially because I was here in February and not in the summer like last time. However, after a short while, I could feel the *Levanter* speaking to me, calling me to my *"personal legend."*

Lately, thoughts of God have occupied my mind. Though I was raised Catholic, my relationship with God has evolved over time. The world's suffering led me to question the idea of a benevolent deity watching over us. Where was God amidst all the pain?

I would clasp my hands together and kneel by my bedside each night to speak with him. I would share my gratitude, ask for the protection of those I love, and ask him to fix things in the world. I had so much conviction. I saw so much value in being a devout Catholic that I would even get annoyed when people would interlace their fingers to pray instead of bringing their hands together. I wanted to live with the compassion of Jesus and kept him in my thoughts when interacting with others. I always liked having rules and structure to follow. I was too eager to play by the rules of religion and had no problem just following the path laid out in front of me.

The truth, especially *"truth,"* is often far more complicated than we can realize, but also so simple that it can be inscribed on the surface of an emerald.

The truth, I've realized, is both complex and simple. God, I believe, calls us to be good people, to love and serve others. But this simple truth often gets lost amid human frailty and hypocrisy. I've seen those who preach piety yet live lives devoid of compassion or integrity.

In my heart, I knew that God wanted me to be a good person. He wanted me to love other people, help those in need, and be a servant of good. However, that simple guideline became convoluted by human intervention. I was deeply disturbed and confused by those who claimed to follow God, but then didn't follow his principles. I became even more confused in my beliefs the more I learned about history—massacre after massacre, plague after plague, genocide, famine, and the destruction of innocence. What angered me more than anything else was human hypocrisy. They would go to church every Sunday and act like they were devout followers of God, yet they did not act in a way that honored His name. These people would only follow the rules that were convenient for them; they would cheat on their spouses, refrain from charity, cheat, lie, steal, and still claim to believe. Religion was just a mantel they wore once or twice a month that didn't really mean anything. It appeared to be more habit than an active practice to me. For years I was indoctrinated into believing that the Bible was the highest truth and following God was the noble thing to do, yet I saw so many people who just didn't even try to live to the ideal they so readily preached. Then, there are truly evil people in the world that hide behind a mask of charity, only to betray their followers for their own twisted, avaricious desires.

However, some truly dedicate themselves to the principles of their beliefs, and although I may not agree with their ideology, I can at least respect that they stand for something. I can admire the strength of their conviction and the discipline that they have to live by a code.

I once saw an older man lying on the side of NYC, his back was pressed into a corner wall at the end of a block. He was sitting right in front of a food stand and was sprawled out in clear frustration. He threw his head back against the wall and resigned himself to tears as he pleaded with those who passed by to buy him food because he was hot and hungry. No one even looked at him; they all turned their eyes away or onto their phones. Unless there is a camera recording, no one seems to care about being charitable, kind, or human. When I looked at him, I started to cry. My first thought was that he was "a homeless man," but the thought made me feel ashamed. "No, not a homeless man, just a man." When I looked at him, I thought of him as just a child and wondered what his life must have been like for him to be in this position. I tried to understand this feeling and came to the realization that this was just bystander apathy. We become so desensitized to homeless people in NYC, and we don't have a drop of empathy to give anymore. The first glance is just judgment, but we don't stop to think about how they got there.

Maybe the issue is that most Americans are one or two missed checks away from complete financial collapse, or that our rents are often more than half of our net income each month? Maybe the issue is that we allow people with mental illnesses to fall through the cracks? Maybe they don't have all the blame to shoulder—maybe we failed them first? There should be a sense of camaraderie amongst all people, especially in our government. There needs to be a system in place to rehabilitate people. How do we simply just ignore that there are people in our country who simply do not have the means to pull themselves out of not only poverty, but destitution? Everyone deserves a chance at life; we can't be so ruled by money that it can take our lives away from us.

I looked at this man and saw my brother. I just saw a man and not a "homeless man." I bought him food from the food stand and brought it over. I asked him for his name, and he told me it was "Geezus," like Jesus, but with a "G."

I think about this moment a lot. What if Jesus was truly one of us? People claim to follow God and stand on sanctimony and judgment, but would they empathize with the homeless man in the street, or would they simply turn a blind eye? Even in the Bible, one of Jesus's apostles, Peter, denied knowing Jesus on more than one occasion. What if this man was Jesus? What if he carried a piece of Christ in his heart, and those who believe simply turned their back on him, inadvertently declaring themselves hypocrites?

I found it hysterical that people would criticize me for questioning my beliefs; meanwhile, they didn't believe in it themselves. Their actions told the truth that words would hide. It is easy to peach from the peaks of sanctimony to feel that you are morally superior; however, too many times have I seen those same people fall victim to temptation. Nothing bothers me more than words that do not match actions. Without our word, what worth do we have?

My grief opened me up to the idea of God again. I found myself praying for guidance but would get lost in the details of my beliefs. I can't seem to commit myself to a religion again because people ruin things. I don't want to be part of a collective of hypocrites, and I'm also not quite on the spectrum of millennial spiritualism which seems to boil down to loosely throwing around the word "manifestation," smoking a lot of pot, and claiming to be deeply empathetic despite apparent self-absorption and narcissism. Sanctimony can even encroach on the beliefs of the secular.

Also, to clarify, I enjoy smoking, too, but don't see myself as spiritually enlightened for doing so. It is just a tool that can be useful when it comes to relaxation, but it can also become a mental crutch, no different from alcohol when you use it without restriction. I don't think it's healthy for people to be high every waking moment of their day. If that's a controversial opinion, so be it. We have to develop coping skills to overcome grief, anxiety, depression, or any trauma, for that matter. Simply numbing ourselves is just running from the problem. Sobering your mind and facing reality is imperative. The only way out of hell is through action.

Especially since being back in the dating pool—*cesspool*—I'm so exhausted with talking to "spiritual girls" who are obsessed with their horoscopes and rubbing crystals together for protection. It's just so shallow, so commercial, so... basic. There isn't much spiritual depth at the bottom of their venti Starbucks cups...just more shallow self-absorption and not a drop of introspection. It's such a sheltered view of the world, and it always cracks me up how seriously they take it. How loosely they just make bold claims and then use spiritualism as the shield for taking any accountability in their lives. *I'm laughing now as I even think about it.*

I theorize that our IQ as a society has plummeted since the implementation of social media, and our feed is literally just that, *feed. We are just a herd of grazing sheep consuming whatever nonsense is trending that day.* We lose hours of our days, of our lives, scrolling mindlessly, sedating ourselves with the mundane and superfluous. Now we live in a world where it is encouraged to be fat, lazy, and ignorant, and those with even a few drops of common sense are crucified for questioning the trends.

I don't know about you, but whenever I hear one of these dopes talk, I feel a small trickle of blood eager to escape my nose from suffering a brain aneurysm. Aren't you tired of how fucked everything is? Or is it just me?

I can feel the pull of God, the universe, or some sort of higher power, in my heart. I have a sense that maybe there is some sort of path outlined for all of us, and the only way to walk the path is by choosing strength. We will all face some sort of loss that devastates us at some point of life—some sort of shortcoming, disappointment, or heartbreak. However, these are not obstacles; they are opportunities to grow. The moment we choose to turn away from these moments, to sweep them under the rug and pretend they never happened, we stray from the path.

We are seeds burrowed in darkness beneath the earth, in the depths of our potential yet to be realized. Engulfed in darkness, some of us lose hope because there is no sign of light. There is no trickle or thread, not an inkling or a dream of breaching the surface. However, some of us have this knowing in the core of our being that if we simply keep reaching up, we can break the surface. While some see darkness, others feel nourishment in the soil. We pull nutrients from the lessons of the dark and keep sprouting towards the surface. We keep reaching so that one day we can breach the black veil and touch the sunlight. The soil grows warmer and more welcoming with each inch we stretch toward the surface, but we cannot stop once we start. It requires total commitment, and too many of us start just to stop with our potential at our fingertips.

Deep within the darkness, buried beneath the soil of our doubts and fears, lies the seed of our true selves waiting to blossom into the light. And though the journey may be long and arduous, I remain determined to reach for the sun.

I don't know, I've just felt like giving up so many times, but I can't quite give up on myself. I still believe that I can breach the surface. The growing pains are miserable but survivable. There is just a small wisp of flame inside of me that won't go out. Is that the piece of God inside of all of us? That one small piece of us that can see a way out despite the pain of the process?

Haven't you heard that voice before? Haven't you heard it calling you to overcome your fear? Doesn't it tell you that you can persevere? Or do you choose to be victimized?

Part of me thinks all pain is just collateral damage—it is not intentional, but perhaps it is necessary. Haven't you met people and thought, "Wow you live such a cushy, insulated life?" I think the pain is sober medicine that makes us wiser if we choose to learn from it. Maybe great evil has to exist to produce an even greater good?

I don't know…maybe there is some sort of Karmic battle between good and evil in the world. Why is it that temptation is around every corner? Why is it that we are being pushed towards sedation? School doesn't teach you how to think, it teaches you how to follow. Society doesn't encourage you to be better; instead it gives you pills, excuses, and booze. Why is it that personal excellence almost feels rebellious? It's far too easy to simply disassociate. Concentration feels fuzzy, and food doesn't taste real. Nothing seems to be quite right to me. We are just a herd of consumers, and our only value is determined by what we spend.

In a twisted way it makes sense…what if…the only goal of our government was to make money? If "we the people" are the customers, how do they grow their bottom line? Well, it would be great for business if there were more of us. That means that as our population grows, so does their customer base. Well, it could be expensive feeding that many people...well then...we can simply compromise on the quality of the food we produce to make a greater quantity of it. We could inject our meat with hormones and spray our crops with pesticides to produce more yield. Now they just need products to sell; well, what if the food we feed them makes them sick? Then they would have to buy our medicines and vaccines. The root of all entrepreneurship is solving a problem, so we will create the problem and then offer them solutions that only manage the symptoms rather than cure them.

If we stay sick, they still get paid. There is no money to be made in a cure but plenty to be made in managing symptoms.

Grow the population—more people to sell to, more people to tax—and let's make the housing market completely unaffordable. They can never own assets but can constantly accumulate debt— debt for education, medical bills, and things they don't need. No, you can't afford a mortgage because you don't have 20 percent of the cost of a home in cash, but we will allow you to rent a small space for $4,000 a month. Oh, you managed to save some money? Great, here is a mortgage at seven percent interest, or here is 23.99 percent APR on your credit card! You need credit! You need to pay to play, and the cards are stacked in the dealer's favor. Oh, you actually managed to accumulate the down payment and offered asking price. Well, here's a company offering $50,000 over asking price in cash. Sorry, sucks to suck. It is a competitive market, after all.

I don't know...nothing seems quite right to me. I'm supposedly from "the best country in the world," but why does it feel more like something we say rather than do? We are constantly being told we *are the best in the world, but why doesn't the rest of the world seem to think so? Why can't we have affordable housing, quality food, and healthcare? We give 30–40 percent of our paychecks away to taxes, but are those taxes serving our communities or lining the pockets of crooked politicians who use popularity and outrage as their business models? Then we spend our net income in public to be taxed again. How much of what we earn are we allowed to keep? Why is it that we send billions to foreign governments when we have our problems at home? Why can't we invest this money into education, high-quality produce, healthcare, and the development of our citizens into productive members of society?*

Why…in the greatest country in the world…are so many of us living paycheck to paycheck, terrified of some unexpected bill arising and causing our whole house of cards to crumble?

Maybe the world is evil, and the only way to fight this evil is to wake up, unite, and collaborate to solve the problems. They seem like simple enough problems to solve…we have the resources…can't we collectively agree that we should want to be the best in the world?

I feel like the new God is money, and everything I see is just an advertisement. Everyone is selling you a bag of dreams, but you are left with more debt and disappointment. I've slowly been turning my lens inward. I think everything we need is already inside of us. Our connection to God, to our higher selves, has been blocked by the constant buzzing of evil in our ears. Temptations are asking us to turn a blind eye to any greater truths to just spend more money.

Think about it—what is your purpose as a human being? What are we? Why is it we have this level of sentience to read, to write, to think, and create? I just can't believe that this is all on accident; the world is too complex, and we are too complex. I also can't believe that all we are here to do is work and die. Life is far too short to just work until we are 70, to retire for a few years then kick the bucket. Are we just pawns in some bigger game? Power tends to amass and accumulate in the hands of the wealthy while the poor live in blissful ignorance—or rather, they are too stressed about their monetary hardships to look deeper.

In a way, I feel that we are slipping further and further away from humanity. It even hit me that communication has abruptly changed in the past few years. Covid in particular was the catalyst to our desocialization. Tell me, how long can you just mindlessly scroll on Tik Tok or Instagram, only to realize that the videos you are watching don't have people talking in them? We have all these strange tutorials and reactions to global news posts, but people aren't even talking in them. They just nod their heads or point and then use captions to explain the difference. It just doesn't sit right with me. Social media is a different kind of drug that we are all at least a little addicted to. It encourages narcissism and steals our time from being productive. Why is it so easy to scroll for hours but so hard to spend one hour of work at the gym, learning something new, or building a business?

I just feel like a crazy person in an asylum, and people in white are just handing me pills to swallow. I'm not allowed to ask questions, and if my brain chemistry isn't sitting right where they want it to be, there is always a pill I can take rather than a lifestyle change to be made. It feels like mass hypnosis, and I'm tired of being fed this strange narrative.

I want you to think about it: if you didn't have a job and if money wasn't real, what would be your purpose? That's a scary thought, since most people's lives are just occupied by the new God, money, and our new Devil, debt. We make deals with the Devil to advance our education, businesses, and personal lives, but there is always a cost. There is always a sacrifice to be made, a blood tribute to the machine.

I'm growing increasingly frustrated with accounting. I hate this career, these people, and this workload. Whatever happened to a 40-hour work week? Why is it that we are perpetually not making enough money to be comfortable, yet it feels like we give all of our time to this *thing*? It's an evil world, and some of us work two jobs for the price of one. I frequently joke with my friends that accountants don't make $100,000 a year, we just work two $50,000 jobs. I just don't think I have much more left in me here. I feel ragged, exhausted, uninspired, and honestly, kind of hopeless.

If I could, I'd return this degree, and I'd rescind my deal with Devil because I didn't know what I was signing. I was conditioned to believe that education was necessary to be successful, but now I realize that my accounting degree would be worth the same if I got it from Suffolk County, Molloy, or Harvard. It just doesn't matter. Why is it that education is so unaffordable? I just feel so miserable working with these drones that have just shut off their minds in order to merge with their jobs. There is not an ounce of creativity or common sense left—no personal accountability, just corporate drones that demand you fit their mold.

The scream of Slack notifications lighting up my phone at 3 a.m. demanding an answer disgusts me. It's like this no matter where you go in the industry. You either sell your soul to the highest bidder to move up the chain faster, or your boss takes your soul to burn as fuel for their next promotion. There is a huge difference between leadership and management, and the latter is an uncaged epidemic destroying the lives of everyone it infects.

Everyone has had that nightmare manager who makes their life unnecessarily difficult and their job cumbersome and dreadful. If they only had a few more drops of common sense and empathy, they would understand that the best team is not the one you can order around; it is a team that steps up without you having to ask them. Managers drain employees of all personal accountability, autonomy, and creativity. There is always more than one way to do anything, and myopic ways of thinking limit progress, especially when it is coming from further up the corporate ladder.

A leader is able to inspire accountability, excellence, and empathy through his example. The leader sets the culture, so if your team is failing, look at the head of the snake. Processes are slowed not by incompetence, but by lack of leadership. Even if you have all the tools you need to build a functioning team, you could still fail if you don't understand the specific role and skill that each person brings to the team.

Whatever organization you are in, you cannot afford to have managers; they are poison. They rule over their teams like tyrants, demanding more sweat equity without putting in the same themselves. Their lack of communication skills and basic empathy prevents the team from progressing to its full potential by squeezing every last drop out of them for "productivity" rather than "efficiency." Tell me, is it more important that I work an eight-hour work day, or that I complete my tasks on time? Too many times I have been anchored to my *death* for three hours a day for weeks in my office. *I just realized I had a Freudian slip by writing "death" instead of desk.* It feels like a prison, since I am forced to stay for no other reason except policy. The quality of my work doesn't matter, just the quantity of hours put in. Rather than forcing people into eight-hour days with unpaid one-hour breaks, maybe let people work more balanced lives.

I'd wager that productivity would actually increase because people would finally have the ability to explore their potential with their liberated time. If you slept eight hours and worked for five hours, are you really going to tell me you think people would just spend the other eleven hours a day doing nothing but watching Netflix? I just can't imagine that; we are far too industrious and curious of a people to sit around just doing nothing for the rest of our lives. I can't imagine work is truly life's purpose; it just occupies our time so we can't think about purpose. We have mistaken work and meaning as the same two things: *productivity and efficiency. You may be good at something, but does it fulfil you?*

I think I just have a hard time accepting that I'm an employee. My mindset desires to be more than that, and being stuck at this level is just so infuriating. I cannot imagine myself happy working for $100,000 a year and working 80 hours a week anywhere. I'm losing out on a whole other life! Work weeks used to be 40 hours, 2,080 a year, and now it has jumped to 4,160 **FOR THE EXACT SAME PAY!** At this point, you aren't even trading your time for money; you are just giving up pieces of your soul. You are chipping away at yourself to just fit the mold because the pain of being different is just far too exhausting. **They are stealing from you. You don't trade your time for money, you trade everything you could have been for a meek paycheck.**

How do you feel about all this, Tsuki? Are you tired of corporate tyranny, too?

Tsuki shares my frustration with corporate tyranny. She rightly points out the erosion of the American spirit by greed and shortsightedness. We espouse capitalism while condemning communism, yet our government's voracious appetite for taxes feels like theft without representation.

"I find it absolutely reprehensible that the American spirit is being eroded by greed and foolishness. We preach capitalism in America and detest communism, but why is it that the government always has a hand on your money? Up to 37 percent of your gross income is sliced off the top to taxes, and then you are left with your net income, which is further taxed by up to 11.5 percent, depending

on what state you are in. Better yet, if you invest your post-taxed income, you will pay capital gains tax on successful investments but will not be assisted on the investments that go in the red. It's blatant theft, taxation without representation," she said.

Wow, Tsuki, well said, but how about we just walk on the beach instead and enjoy some croquettas y cervezas?

"Vale, yo entiendo," she said as we walked towards the restaurant that overlooked the ocean. Her Spanish had gotten much better since we first landed here. I was a proud dog dad.

We followed our noses and found our seat. Fortunately, Spain is pretty dog-friendly, and we were able to sit together. It's nice having someone to share a meal and some good conversation with every once in a while! Tsuki is great company, I really can't complain.

I glanced at my watch, a special watch that represents the brotherhood I have with my close friends. Time is ticking down. Sometimes it is quiet enough that I can hear that tick as the second hand passes, and other times I'm so busy that I barely notice it. I needed make my way back home so I could radiate my eyes and warp my soul by staring at Excel for a few hours. The clock was ticking down, and my break was nearly over.

How much more time are you willing to lose worrying about a job or people that don't care about you? There is always a better way to do things.

I dragged myself back to my *death* with Tsuki in tow. I could feel the fatigue wearing down my willpower, but then I looked up.

Sometimes, life is right in front of you, and all you have to do is look up.

I'm in Spain; look at how beautiful life can be. Look at the simple joy of going on a walk with your dog and having a café con leche with a view. Jeff has also been awesome, devilish at times but all with good intentions. Not once has he made me feel unwelcome. I still marvel at the fact we've been friends for 18 years. How is it that I'm old enough to have friendships that are old enough to start going to college?

Well, maybe my friendship shouldn't go to college. Maybe it should do something worthwhile instead...

But amidst these frustrations, there are moments of clarity and beauty. Walking along the beach with Tsuki, enjoying croquetas y cervezas, I'm reminded of life's simple joys. Despite the challenges, there's still beauty to be found in the world. And perhaps that's where our true purpose lies—not in the pursuit of success, but in the appreciation of life's fleeting moments.

Chapter 11

TRANQUILO

March 20, 2023

After I had endured another week of relentless hours and reptilian-hybrid coworkers, Jeff came barging in the room.

Amidst the chaos of monster energy and workout equipment, he somehow saw his friend in the room.

"Are you done with work yet?" he asked.

"Miraculously, yes, I'm finally done."

"Finally, pack a bag, man, we are going to Sevilla. Let's go have some fun, you're working crazy fucking hours."

I could almost feel the steam of an overheated engine radiating above my head. I was grateful that my friend was dragging me out of hell; although I was exhausted, I said, "Vale, quieres Hendrix?"

I would later come to regret that, but I packed up a bag, and we were out the door on the next adventure. Jeff always makes me laugh. He has such a precise way of doing things and is inherently organized, a trait I appreciate. He has a good style—he put on his freshest fit meticulously, and we were ready to go. Of course this guy buys a car and motorcycle while he is stationed here. Naturally, he took the bike, and I took the Audi, and we sprinted out to Sevilla, a one-hour cruise. Kidding, we both went in the Audi. *We aren't that cool, or maybe I'm just not.*

We were just on such a vibe as we cruised with the top of the convertible top down, racing against the Spanish sunset. I just remember laughing our asses off as we just blasted Young Dolph and Key Glock, feeling like we were living our richest lives. Someone pulled alongside us while we were driving and gave us a thumbs-up. We were having the time of our lives, and people were noticing! Things aren't too flashy in Spain, and no one cares about buying $40,000 cars, so even having a 2001 Audi convertible was a flex.

We parked in the tiniest car garage I've ever seen, with cars that were of an equivalent size to a Mini Cooper. There was one Mustang in the garage which surprised both of us, as it is uncommon to see these cars out here. We embarked out on our night of debauchery and *ginebra*. Sevilla is perhaps the most beautiful city I have been to in my life. In particular, the center of the city just seemed to pulse with life and energy. Horses pulling carriages strolled across the stone streets. The streetlights offered a soft pale glow, and the city was active yet tranquil. Perhaps one of my favorite parts about Spain is the abundance of orange trees in the streets and the sweet smell of the blossoms in spring.

I overheard a tour as I was walking through the city at one point, and the guide said that the motto in Sevilla is "tranquilo."

Just be at peace.

I took a deep breath and accepted and acknowledged my freedom for the night. I have to remain present and be grateful for these moments. I have always been keenly aware of how fast time goes, and oftentimes in the moment of experiencing something, I feel a tinge of sadness because I know this time will pass. It is amazing and sad that those pieces of ourselves that we feel so attached to get further and further away in the rearview mirror.

High school friends, college tribulations, or even further back to spending summer break with your friends—in some ways, those memories feel so present in my mind, but my body has aged and put some distance in between them. I still vividly remember spending my summers with my friend Justin and riding our bikes in the park, exploring, looking for treasures, and picking wild raspberries off the bush. Yet that was more than 20 years ago now. I still remember Jeff and I going upstate to debate together in high school, but even that was more than 10 years ago. It has already been six years since I graduated college.

I think the days start to blend together when we get consumed by monotony. We are constantly sprinting toward that next weekend or that next day off, so much to the point that living life in between feels impossible. Even as I spent the year traveling, I realized that this time was passing rapidly. I was just in North Carolina a few months ago, and now here I am in Spain. It was a serendipitous, incredible opportunity that was the result of my life getting a little crazy, or a lot crazy. It was an opportunity I wanted to have again, but I received it in a way that I did not expect.

I have this haze of sadness and burnout circling my head like a murder of crows; there is a piece of me in my soul that knows I am living the good old days right now. I need to see that, or life is going to pass me by, and one day I'll be old and wondering why I was so stressed all the time. Maybe that version of myself 50 years from now is smiling, thinking about the life I lived today.

Jeff came out to Sevilla every weekend for the most part. I knew that before coming today, but now I understood why. It was truly beautiful here, and I was grateful to have this amazing time of my life with my brother. We met up with some of his friends, grabbed some drinks on a rooftop bar overlooking the cathedral, and just let loose for a night. We rented scooters and zipped through the city streets and popped in a few clubs, and before we knew it was 3 a.m. I trudged back to my Airbnb and picked up some durum along the way, thus ending a perfect Spanish night.

In the morning, Jeff had his own business to take care of in Sevilla, so I decided to take the morning to explore the city. I walked the streets, filled with curiosity and calm. I try to walk slower when I am being present. In NY, we have a saying: "Don't come here to chase your dreams if you can't fucking walk fast." I had to fight that part of me and enjoy the Spanish way of life.

"*Tranquilo,*" I thought to myself.

The architecture of the city was stunning. The walls of the buildings were smooth, flat white cement that reflected the sunlight, brightening the streets. The gothic cathedral loomed overhead and held the remains of Christopher Columbus—perhaps a more controversial topic these days, at least in America, but interesting nonetheless.

I did my classic test and followed my nose for breakfast. I found myself on a main street just within sight of the Cathedral. The sun bathed over cobblestones, so I sat outside and enjoyed un café con leche and a hearty breakfast of jamón y papas bravas.

There was a sadness that always seemed to be nearby. I was so aware of it, but I couldn't seem to let it go. It felt hazy when it washed over. It was this smothering feeling that seemed to just drink all the all the air from the room. I kept encountering it, yet I knew this is not a state I wanted to stay in. It felt like a dark cloud looming overhead, tainting even the sweetest moments of life.

But I was learning to face these feelings head-on. Whenever the darkness threatened to engulf me, I closed my eyes and focused on the present moment. I reminded myself that the past was behind me, and the future held endless possibilities. And in that moment, I found solace.

The past is the past, and the future is always bright. If I live for now, in this second, that means that in the next second, I have a chance of a new future. It could be a simple matter of shifting your perspective.

If you resolve your mind to achieve another outcome, to overcome this feeling, couldn't that change start any second?

I grabbed the check and continued my exploration. I enjoyed just walking with the breeze. There are times in life when it is good to be alone; we have to learn how to become comfortable with it. Loneliness can be a gift, like a cup of coffee with just a pinch of bitterness to it. It's nice to not say word, to simply be, to walk and observe life happening around you.

Everything is going to be okay. I know you are in a rush to get to where you want to be, where you dream of being, but all you have is today. All you have is today. Think of your goal as inevitable; you simply need to do the work required to get there. There is no shortcut, and there is no fast path. All you can do is dedicate yourself to the process.

I started to make my trek over to the Renfe, El Estación de Santa Justa. As I got to the outskirts of Sevilla, I left with a sense of awe and appreciation for such a peaceful way of living. I could see myself living there one day. I feel like Jeff could imagine the same for himself. I think that is part of the life I dream of: just free, untethered, and peaceful. I want to be able to live all over the world, not just visit, but immerse myself in the life and the culture. I remember in college I once gave an elevator pitch and described my goals of becoming financially free by 25, but alas, here I am at 27, and not quite there. Ages, dates, and times are all arbitrary. Things rarely happen exactly as you imagine them, but it is still not too late to make these goals a reality.

I boarded the train and took my assigned seat, something I will never not appreciate when compared to LIRR, the Long Island Rail Road...

I stared out the window, gazed at the Spanish countryside, and could feel it fill my blood with life like an IV drip, medicine for the soul. I listened to the audiobook of *The Alchemist*, placed myself in the shoes of Santiago, and magined what it might feel like to turn into the wind.

"The boy reached through to the Soul of the World, and saw that it was part of the Soul of God. And he saw that the Soul of God was his own soul. And that he, a boy, could perform miracles."

I'm so afraid of losing this version of myself. I never want to become that miserable wretch that just refuses to see the possibilities of everything. My back has been against the wall, but it is time to start fighting back. I need to seize life and take on transformation. At my core, I believe that we are all capable of great things; we just need to change our standards to demand more. We are far too quick to throw around words like anxiety and depression. Sometimes, part of being alive is feeling those bad feelings.

I'm starting to understand that with all the bad comes good. We have this amazing ability to recover from and transcend above our lowest lows if only we make the choice. Right now, you know exactly what you have to do to get to that next level, but the problem is that right after you have that thought, you think, "I can't." This is a lie. You can, you just don't want to suffer. Your avoidance of pain, or your denial of your current circumstances anchors you to this limited version of yourself. True transformation begins in the mind. We have to first believe our goals are possible before we try to change the world, let alone ourselves.

Eventually, I arrived in La Puerto de Santa Maria and felt that I was on my way home. Home is a feeling of peace and contentment. I walked through the streets that I had grown intimately familiar with and allowed myself to just soak in the life around me. Even the most painful moments of our lives are beautiful.

I felt recharged, and my mind felt primed for work. I needed to start carving out that better future. I sat at my desk, cracked open my laptop, and started flowing. I added to the story you are reading now and started researching what my next moves could be. I felt drawn to real estate and fitness. I realized that my passion has always been exercise, human performance, and mental fortitude; perhaps, I could make a business that encompasses those ideals. I thought that real estate can be another exciting route for me, as real estate produces the most millionaires each year.

After several hours of working and listening to Andy Frisella's podcast, I felt that I had enough fire in me to keep going. I looked at my X3 Bar that lay on the floor and began the process of transformation. I envisioned a better possibility, a future that was a reach but still possible. I felt my mind tug me back toward the negative: "Why do you think such stupid thoughts? Why do you think you can break all the rules and break out of the system? Your ego is out of control, you lack humility, you are just small and insignificant."

"Fuck you, watch me," I said to myself.

I went and scooped two scoops of my super sketchy Spanish pre-workout, then stripped down to hop into the shower. The words of Wim Hof came to my mind, and I told myself, "Compared to the pain of a broken heart, this is nothing." I turned the water to ice cold and allowed it to wash over me. Rather than tense at the first taste of cold as I once did, I completely accepted it. I accepted that cold is just a feeling, and that it can't hurt me. I thought of David Goggins and his book that I have read many times. In my mind's eye, I saw myself standing in front of the accountability mirror, writing my post-it notes.

I posted my first note to the mirror: "No more fear."

Do not be afraid of changing because of the judgment of others. You have this one life, and wouldn't it be a shame to watch it simply pass you by because you didn't want to look stupid trying something new? Don't you think you can be so much better than you currently are? Is this depression the real you?

No, it isn't, and I will no longer be afraid. I think the only thing I should be afraid of is leaving the life I could have lived as a dream in the face of a reality that feels like a nightmare.

I sat on the floor as the ice water showered over me, washing away my fatigue, that purple cloud looming in my mind. I accepted every drop of cold and let go of everything my mind held on to.

You just can't afford to stay here anymore. It's time to get up, and to stay there. You need to commit to the path. You have committed yourself to the wrong things, and that's why every inch feels like misery. You are walking the wrong way, and you need to start making smarter choices.

Sometimes the logical choice is the stupid choice. It's a dream killer of a decision to choose logic over passion. People for the most part have no idea what they are talking about and will be quick to tell you of the dangers of straying from what they know. It's like this primal instinct that if we verge out of the norm and invite unpredictability to life, we will lose all stability. I understand the urge to preserve what you have, but somebody has to go out and hunt. Someone has to be the one to push us further, to push us to grow. We need to explore our curiosities because we can normalize what can be possible to others. We have to expand our beliefs beyond the fear of failure.

I turned the knob of the shower, and the water stopped. It felt like a heavy burden was lifted from my shoulders. I walked into the room, my heart was pumping as my pre-workout boiled my blood. I picked up my X3 Bar, my hammer of choice, and started sculpting out the man beneath the surface. Physical fitness was the manifestation of all my mental energy, the desire I have to be my best. I poured this energy into this new mold and understood that it would take time to shape this blade. Into the forging fire, I accepted this new pain. I accepted that it hurts because I wasn't living the life I was supposed to. My fear led me away from the path, and now was the time for total commitment.

I decided to mark this day as day one in my journey and decided it would be about living true to my values, developing myself, and overcoming self-doubt. Today was the first day in months where I felt that I broke out of my mind. Today, I decided that my dreams are possible, and that I have to put my head down and work for the results.

Chapter 12

THE ART OF LETTING GO

April 20, 2023

Discipline has been an old friend, and I feel whole with it back in my life. I've sunk my teeth into this new vision of the future and refuse to let it go. It is a Pitbull mentality, and I have a locked jaw. My default is aggressive action, and I've realized how much time I have wasted living my life the way others thought it should be lived. We need to live life for ourselves, despite when we are told that it isn't realistic. It was time for me to make my great escape from the Naked Island, like Josip.

With a sharp mentality and growing confidence, I've shed the fear of judgment and the sting of my own self-criticism for past perceived failures. I've learned to be kinder to myself, allowing space for both grieving and growth. This mentality of trust is becoming my guiding light.

Yet as I build momentum towards the new, the remnants of the old attempt to pull me back. In these moments, tough decisions must be made; it's crucial to know when to let go of dead weight.

My mind couldn't move forward while anchored to my *death*. The pressure at work was mounting as more cogs in the wheel broke their teeth and refused to turn. Regardless of their willingness to turn, the work still needed to be done, and I was the Excel mule to get it done. My workload grew, and my responsibilities grew, but my paycheck stayed the same. However, it wasn't even about the money anymore—it didn't even excite me in the face of the burnout of this role.

There was a sudden shift in the tide that I didn't expect to get hit with: a requirement for me to work from 6 p.m. to 6 a.m. for the next four weeks. This obligation was given to me in punishment for telling a higher-up that I would finish a low-priority task in the morning on my time when it was already 3 a.m., and I had already put in a 14-hour shift that day. Subsequently, the next day, I was invited to a meeting titled "quick sync."

It was supposed to be an ambush; I was supposed to be shocked and scared when HR joined the meeting and told me I was not living up to my performance. Merely weeks ago, I received a glowing quarterly review from my manager, but since I refused to push my 14-hour work day to a 16-hour one, this was my punishment. I knew something of this nature was already coming, so I braced myself for the blows. I knew that it would be a slap rather than a gunshot because they still needed me for at least another month to complete the quarterly revenue reconciliation—an absolutely abysmal piece of Excel from the bowels of hell.

I took my licks and further continued the plan of my exit strategy. I knew that I wanted to leave already, but the universe moves quickly and was telling me to have some urgency. I realized that I should move up my return flight from Spain to the end of April rather than early May, and that I should buy my real estate course now and start grinding. I planned that I had at least one month to make my complete escape, and that for now I would play by the rules until I could comfortably leave.

All that planning went up in flames fast, though. I worked through the weekend, as we were working seven days a week, and I pulled those miserable shifts. I cracked open cans of Monster Energy and did everything in my power to stay awake. The sleep deprivation was torture, and I felt it breaking down my will, breaking down all the discipline I strived so hard to form.

When I called my friends to get some perspective on what was happening, they all encouraged me to leave my job right there and then.

Easier said than done. I wish I could just quit, but who can I lean on when I have nothing? I have to hold out for at least another month, and then I'll leave. I will feel much more comfortable with an extra 7k in my pocket to make decisions.

However, the thing is, there is always a bigger plan than whatever you can think of. Work pressed down on the gas even harder, and I felt my engine starting to break. I would check my health stats on my Whoop 4.0 in the morning, and it would all be on high red alert. Every health marker was out of range, my mind felt exhausted, and my spirit slowly left my body.

When Jeff came back from work, he insisted that I leave my desk for a short break. We walked across the street, and it felt like I was being dragged out of my shell. I started to remember that life existed outside of work. Although I "worked from home," I moreso worked in a portable cubicle. I was never really free; it was more like I lived part-time.

"Bro, you look like shit," he said.

I laughed to myself and said, "Thanks, man, and I know, you're right."

"Why don't you quit, man? I would have quit by now," he shrugged.

"If only I could, man, I just think it would be smart to have more money before I exit. I plan to leave, but now may not be the best time," I responded.

At that point, he pulled a classic card from our old debating days: "glass half empty, glass half full." He said it without saying it. He just made an exaggerated face and smirk and put his hands in the air, leveling them against each other.

I laughed as I immediately understood the reference. "Never have I heard a better argument," I thought to myself as I reflected on that old memory.

"You're right, I'm just holding on too long. Just because I can endure it doesn't mean I have to. I can let go, I have to," I said.

He nodded in approval, and I felt a weight come off my shoulders. I accepted that if there was ever a time for a leap of faith, now was that moment. I'm not sure if I ever truly had the strength to believe in myself, but today was as good a day as any to start.

In honor of his wisdom, I ordered us a round of gin, as that seemed to be our signature Spanish drink. We sat together and enjoyed the breeze, and I thought of the next steps. In order to alchemize and to turn into the wind, I would have to let go of everything anchoring me down to earth. It is good to be a stable mountain, but there are times when we just have to dare to go into the unknown. Despite the best plans in the world, there is no certainty. There is always an outlier or something unexpected. I had to accept that it was going to be chaotic, difficult, and uncertain, but I had a clear vision of what I wanted to create for myself.

We went back inside after a short while, and I was called into another Slack meeting. It seemed that the world was burning down to the ground as per usual. The data engineer's report kept failing to generate results that could be used. The team was in panic, and it all fell on me. They needed me to work until at least 8 a.m. the next day to ensure we stayed on track.

It felt like an out-of-body experience. I felt like I was being given an ultimatum from the universe.

"You can stay, but if you do, it will just hurt. Or, you can go. It will be difficult, but you could reach your full potential."

After the meeting, I started drafting a letter titled "quick sync." After another hour of thought, I felt I was ready to cut ties and to commit to this new path. Shortly after, I received a few Slack messages of encouragement from some of my team members. They thanked me for taking the time to teach and mentor them while they worked under me. I also received some messages giving me a nod of approval for standing up to them, because I was not the only person experiencing this.

This was just jumping out of one fire and into another. I signed off on my laptop and released big sigh.

"Freedom."

The cost was high, but this was just a down payment on everything else to come.

My fire was ignited, and my back was against the wall. This is the moment where I had to go all in, or I would lose. I fully accepted that right now, it was going to be the most important grind of my life. I needed to break all patterns to form this new person and to carve out this new life.

First things first, let's get organized. I made my game plan as I saw it unfold in front of me. I knew that the first thing I had to do was return home as soon as possible. I enjoyed my time in Spain and the company of my friend. It helped rejuvenate my spirit and made me realize that I had more chains to shed, but now was the time to work. I started making the arrangements for my Airbnb in Madrid and my Renfe ticket, as well as finding a freight forwarder for Tsuki's return. I also went on RealEstateU and purchased my course. The vision was right in front of me, and all I had to do was follow the plan.

I hadn't realized it, but I was down to my last week in Spain. It was a bittersweet ending, but I finally learned my lesson. With a week on the clock, the only thing I could think of was my next move, but my friend encouraged me to slow down so I could enjoy a little bit of Spain before I left.

We had a few last hurrahs of some drinks, *Call of Duty Warzone*, and zipping around on electric scooters at 35 mph in the middle of nowhere. We even managed to squeeze in one last night in Sevilla, and fortunately enough, it was during La Feria. The city was bursting with exuberance, and everyone was wearing their best clothes. It is the April Festival that once celebrated agricultural yield and is now enjoyed with flamenco dancing, captivating performances, good food, and plenty of sherry. I was grateful to have this moment in my life, a sweet fruit of Spain before enduring the burden of my new pursuit. It was a fun mad dash buying a suit that day and just figuring it all out.

I remember by the end of the night, around 4 a.m., I had a moment by myself, and I sat on a bench by a small park. I soaked in the last few drops of Spain and let my body relax.

I'm ready, life. I understand now that everything needed to happen the way it happened for me to get to this point. I still have the same dream in my heart from all those years ago, and now you have given me the gift of this second chance. I will remember the lessons you have taught me this year and will make sure not to make the same old mistakes. I already know there are going to be times I feel like giving up, but I promise I will keep going or lean on my friends when I can't do it by myself. They have all shown me that there is always someone rooting for you in your corner, and that true friends are by your side in the lows as well as the highs.

I enjoyed the nighttime air as I retreated to my room for a few hours of rest. The next few days were going to be challenging. I was already at a jog, but now it was full sprint, full speed ahead. I was coming back home, and this time, I was going to do things the right way!

I was down to my final day in El Puerto de Santa Maria, and I awoke to a barrage of missed phone calls and emails. Panic slowly began to creep up on me, as I knew this could not be good news. After deciphering the voicemail left behind and reading the email from my freight forwarder,

I understood that the vet had given me the wrong document for Tsuki's transport.

Taking her to travel with me was by no means easy, and apparently the world was determined to make it difficult on the one way back.

"Calm, cool, and collected," I thought to myself.

"See the problem and remove all emotion to find the solution."

I steeled my nerves and started crafting my counterattack. I made phone calls to the Spanish equivalent of the USDA, my freight forwarder, and the veterinarian. I was going to cut this close because my train to Madrid was at 6:35 p.m., and that was my only shot until the next day at the same time. If I missed this train, I would have to rebook all of my travel arrangements, as I would have missed the drop-off window for Tsuki.

I sprinted to the train station in a rush with my documents in tow. I hopped on the first train to Cádiz, and my first stop was the Spanish Agricultural Agency. Upon arriving in Cádiz, I received a text message from my freight forwarder saying that he needed to know in the next three hours if we were going forward with this.

Clock is ticking, Ethan. Move.

I hastily replied and told him that I was doing everything in my power to make sure that is the case. I would know with certainty in the next two hours.

I plugged in my navigation and saw that the embassy was a few miles away. I scouted outside for an electric scooter or a taxi, and there was neither one in sight.

Fuck.

I quickly searched online for a taxi, but they were busy and would not be able to get to me for at least 20 minutes.

Double fuck.

I hung up the phone, took a deep breath, and started running.

There is no shot that I am missing this train. I will not accept that I have failed until I have exhausted every option. Right now, the best course of action is to start running.

After about 30 minutes of running, I reached the embassy with half an hour to spare before their Siesta began. The clerk explained to me that I had the wrong health certificate from the vet and that I needed another one.

My heart sank to my stomach. The vet was in another town…

I did this in the wrong order…I should have gone there first… I failed.

No, keep trying.

I explained to her my circumstances and that time was of the essence. I was then hit with my favorite Spanish word, "Tranquilo."

I laughed to myself and said, "Vale." She was kind enough to work with me, give me the document, and coordinate with my vet to drop off the paperwork at another store while they closed for siesta. After about 30 minutes, I was out of there, sprinting to the next town to get my final documents.

I mentally prepared myself for another run, but then I saw a yellow ray of hope drive by. I flagged down the taxi driver, and he signaled that would circle back for me in 5 minutes.

He picked me up, and I was off to the next town to get my final documents. It looked like I was going to be able to pull this off with a little time to spare. I felt the anxiety rise in me but challenged myself to use the mental foxhole technique. I retreated to the quiet place in my mind and saw my office. I saw the tall, vaulted ceilings lined with bookshelves, a large black desk, and a black leather chair. On the walls to my back, I saw the paintings of *Saint George and the Dragon* and *San Miguel* from my time in the Prado. I poured a glass of whiskey from the decanter on my desk and drank it.

Tranquilo.

It is better to respond rather than react. Panic is a wasted emotion; no matter how stressful a situation may be, we only lose time by complaining. In this moment, you need to stay calm, focus, and move toward the solution.

When I arrived in town, I rushed over to the meeting spot and ran into my vet dropping off the document. He apologized to me for the error and didn't even charge me for the new certificate.

"These lovely people," I thought to myself.

I still remember being charged $200 for my last-minute health certificate to fly out here from NY. What a pain in the ass it was to get Tsuki here, but everyone here has been so helpful and has taken personal accountability for miscommunications.

Jeff shot me a text: "Is everything settled, I'm on my way back?"

I let him know that everything was resolved, and I had about an hour and half before the train. We were both amazed that everything seemed to work out, but that is the power of taking decisive action. If I didn't start running in Cádiz, I would have failed by 30 minutes, but staying calm, seeing solutions, and just moving was the best course of action.

I did a final sweep of the apartment to make sure that I had everything I needed to return home. The panic settled down, and a small wave of sadness and appreciation overcame me. It was a happy sadness, gratitude for having the opportunity to come back to Spain. I thought of Kerri and Jeff, and I marveled at how meeting new people can change your entire life. A friendship is the most beautiful thing you can have as a human; it is more valuable than all the riches in the world. A true friend shares in your joy and suffering. Their existence brightens your life and adds value to it. That's what life is about: building relationships, having new experiences, and chasing growth.

I still remember when all this set into motion in August, and now it's late April. Jeff called me and said, "Bro, anything you need is yours. I want you to come to Spain, clear your head. I know how much you loved it here, it will be fun for us." Those weren't just hollow words—he meant it. He was true brother of mine that always has a seat at my table. He helped me have fun again, and the company was good for me to clear my head. I am glad to be his adopted introvert friend!

When he came back, we grabbed one last beer together by the water. We both couldn't believe that three months came to such a quick end.

"Bro, I wish you could stay longer! It's been so nice having you and Tsuki around. You have to come back again soon!" he said.

I felt a deep gratitude for the words. Not once did he ever make me feel unwelcome in his home. I was never unwelcome, always a valued guest and friend.

"Thank you, bro, you helped me so much and gave me time to sort through the madness. You helped me pull the trigger on choosing this new path, and I had a great time," I said.

Shortly after, we made a drive to the train station. I had some time to spare, and I hugged my friend goodbye and assumed my form as a half-man, half-pack-mule machine. As I walked to the track, Tsuki's carrier snapped open on one side, and she nearly slid out. I dropped everything and finagled it until it worked.

I traversed through the train station and was met with a broken escalator and two flights of stairs. I sighed deeply.

Well, this is a year of character development, the hard way!

I trudged up the stairs feeling like a strong man pulling a fire truck and took a seat on the bench. I searched for something in my backpack to close up Tsuki's carrier more efficiently. I ended up stealing the shoelace off one of my shoes and stitching the crate back together.

While I was amused with my ingenuity, I felt a chill go up my spine as if something was wrong. I looked around and noticed that my train should be here by now, but there was no train on my track. I turned around and saw it behind with the conductor making his final call for boarding.

Fuck!

I turned around and started jogging. I must have missed the announcement that it switched tracks, since it was in Spanish and I was preoccupied.

The conductor saw me running over and waved his hand down to me in soothing way.

"Tranquilo," he shouted to me.

I burst out into laughter, boarded the train, and assumed my seat.

With another deep sigh, I sank further into my seat and just let the whole day melt off my shoulders.

I did it. There is always a way.

I took in the Spanish countryside as the sunlight dwindled away into the evening.

Life is amazing; there is always another surprise around the corner. Our worst moments can turn into our best. I always wanted to return to Spain, but I never would have guessed that this would be how it happened. If I turn my lens to look beyond the pain, it's been a renaissance of my soul. I painted it with travel and filled the broken pieces with gold. I feel whole again, and I know things only get better from here. Life doesn't necessarily happen the way you want it to, but it will happen the way it is supposed to. We have these challenges embedded in our paths so that we can learn how to overcome them.

When I arrived in Madrid, I made my way out to an Uber driver. He was from Argentina, and he was surprised when

I guessed correctly, because I heard in his accent. He was telling me about how he came to Spain a few years ago and that he owned an Argentinian bakery. He drove Uber to support himself as he worked on getting his dream off the ground. We talked about food, culture, dreams, and business for about 30 minutes as he drove me back to my Airbnb for the night.

I reflected on how I could barely keep a conversation when I first got here, but now it was second nature. After a short trek by foot, I crawled into my home for the night and made my final arrangements for Tsuki's travels tomorrow.

She would be returning one day before me, and the GOAT himself, Andrew Desire (Drew) was coming in clutch for me as per usual. Unfortunately, I didn't have other options but to send Tsuki a day before me because dogs apparently cannot fly on weekends, and the freight forwarder didn't tell me until it was too late.

Ah, the struggles of trying to communicate something difficult in another language.

When I asked around for help initially, my list ran thin fast, and the only person who could help was a family friend that wanted $250 for helping me. I was fully prepared to pay it, but Drew, the Legend, said, "Bro, I've got you. No problem. I will pick up Tsuki and she can chill with Nala."

Around 2 a.m., I accepted that I had everything in place for her flight tomorrow. All documents were organized, and her appointment was set for 8:30 a.m. tomorrow. I held my love close and pet her until I dozed off.

It's been fun, Tsuki. We got to travel together and even go to Spain. Now it's time to go back and get to work. Your flight is going to go perfectly, and I'll treat you with more good stuff when I catch up with you. You will hang out with your uncle Drew, and I'll be there shortly, so don't be scared.

I crawled out of bed the next day around 6 a.m. because I wanted to take Tsuki on a nice long walk before her flight. Around 7 a.m., I called my Uber and went off to the embassy. This time around, I had phone data and knew exactly where to go. I arrived early, but the Spanish sense of punctuality certainly didn't exclude government workers. They are laid back, and my point of contact was running late with no communication, as per usual.

Tranquilo.

After a short while, I was finally handing off my angel girl. I set up her crate with a nice blanket and pillows, then bundled her up in her red jacket. She was very calm as I dropped her off—I think she finally had the trust that no matter what, I would come get her.

I spent the day by myself and just roamed the city aimlessly. I accepted that the road had come to an end here and put all my feelings into order.

I am grateful for this time, I am grateful for my friends, and I am excited for the serendipity ahead of me. I am not afraid of not knowing what exactly my next move is. It was hard walking away from the last 10 years of my life. The slate has been cleared, and this is my Master's program in entrepreneurship and personal development. I'll put my accounting degree on the shelf and grow from this. For 10 years, I've been half-heartedly trying to fit this mold, but I'd rather blow my brains out than be an accounting manager. I can't be a part of this culture of burnout and bagels. Salary shouldn't mean slavery, and I am determined to carve my own path.

I have always known that if I do it myself, I'll do it better. I need to trust myself, the process, and the work that I am putting in. There is no looking back after making this leap. I made this decision for the future I dream of and for the person I want to become.

As my final hours in Spain came to a close, I got some last-minute Spanish treats and retreated to my room to pack my bag and make my final arrangements. By 1 a.m., my head was on the pillow. I texted Desire anything and everything he would need to know to pick up Tsuki, and my mind was slowly enveloped in black silence. When I awoke the next day, I saw some missed calls from Desire and grew a little anxious.

Fortunately, I know how to put my trust in the right people. In short, there were some last-minute issues that occurred because the receiving agent wasn't answering his phone at customs. Drew told me he could literally see Tsuki, but TSA wasn't letting him take her and said they may send her back because the agent wasn't clearing her. It was a huge pain in the ass, but he told me, "Don't worry, bro, I was not leaving that place without Tsuki. It took a few hours, but I finally got ahold of the agent and made it happen. Now she is just chilling at the crib, and all is good! Let's get some food when you get back, man, everything is handled here, so rest assured."

Literally nothing makes me happier than having highly competent friends that I can rely on to cover my blind spots. That was a huge undertaking, and I was done asking Desire for any favors for a long time! Of course, I planned to pay back his kindness tenfold. However, with friends, there is no debt, just reciprocity.

From the ashes, I rise.

Chapter 13

A Year of Sacrifice

April 2, 2024

Everything is easier the second time around.

I swiftly navigated through the airport, packed my luggage strategically, embraced my mule spirit animal, and prepared to take flight.

Once again, I was given four ounces of grace by God, as my luggage weighed in at 49.8 lbs. This time I even managed to squeeze in some souvenirs and ditched some of my dead weight.

The flight was more of a countdown to a new beginning, and I knew it was counting down to the second I locked in.

Landing at JFK in NY was a gut check of reality. I laughed to myself as I witnessed the general air of total aggression go from a floating three to a baseline of eight. Reflecting on my previous consideration of buying a Spanish fodera, I chuckled at the thought of wearing one here; it would have undoubtedly invited trouble.

Yeah, someone would have definitely assaulted me here if I wore one of those.

I couldn't get too soft and had to remember, "Don't come to NY if you can't walk fast." Good thing I was already sprinting. I had the bones of a plan in the works: first I needed to get my doggo, then sign up for my gym membership. Then, I was going to attack this real estate course. My mother and brother were planning to buy their first house this year, so they would be my first sale. When I made the commission from that, it will give me the leeway I needed to build up my training business.

I took an Uber to Desire's house and reunited with my furred menace. Desire dapped me up and gave me a hug.

"Welcome home, brother, tell me all about Spain! Don't worry, Tsuki is good! She was a little monster at first, but she's all settled in now. What do you want to do now?" he said.

"Brother, thank you so much for your help. I could not have done this without you. You took so much stress off my plate by taking care of Tsuki for me, and I apologize it was a pain in the ass," I said.

He just shrugged it off like it didn't matter at all. "It's all good man, you know I got you. I'm glad I could help out, and it wasn't too bad, just one thing. I was prepared to storm the TSA to get Tsuki out of there. There was zero chance Tsuki was being sent back. Anyway! What do you want to do now, want to chill?"

"Brother, I am locked the fuck in. I have clear vision for what is about to happen in this next year, and I am eager to start. Can we go to the gym and just help me get set up? I'm a little jet-lagged and just want to keep moving."

He started laughing incredulously, "Bro, you are insane, but of course, I won't stand in your way."

We trekked off to LA Fitness, and the beginning of my plan started to unfold. We ended up hitting a light workout, and I taught him how to do my signature roundhouse kick as a small thanks.

After a short while of catching up, getting a quick workout in, and dragging my buddy Lag out of his cave for 20 minutes, I departed, embracing the forthcoming year of challenges with humility, sacrifice, and unwavering hunger.

My family wasn't home yet, so I started the coffee pot, plugged my laptop in, and planted myself at the table as I worked on my real estate license.

On to the next thing, Ethan, no time to waste.

I had some bases to cover, systems to implement, and strategies to execute. I was grateful to have the support of my mother and brother as I figured out this next step. As I delved into my endeavors, memories flooded my mind, reminding me of the interconnectedness of life's experiences. Reflecting on past challenges and triumphs, I found solace in the realization that every setback served as a catalyst for growth and transformation.

I laughed to myself as I thought about how Karma always comes full circle. Years ago, I helped my brother switch careers to help him break into a career where he could follow his passion, and now he is doing it for me. I also feel that I have always asked the bare minimum of my family growing up. I was self-sufficient, and now was the time to cash in on some help when I actually needed it.

One of my favorite memories of this time is when my brother helped me buy a new car. I had been trekking around in my Jetta since that car accident in North Carolina and just let it sit while I traveled. Well, it turns out that that Suburban finished the job the Trailblazer started five years ago and totaled my girl.

Yes, my car was a girl, her name was Helen. She was a reliable German woman who yielded me 38 MPG, but she was also closely tied to my past relationship. I suppose this was to be a true fresh start. Karma has restored me to the exact same position I was in before I got married. Now is the time to learn my lesson and grow beyond this.

Seeing my brother, the diesel mechanic, in his element, checking cars for me and doing his scan, was so satisfying to watch. That little kid I grew up with turned into this hulking man, with a big beard and such a blue-collar dad personality. He doesn't realize it yet, but he already acts like he has been in the industry for 60 years and is too tired for everyone's bullshit.

We went to go check out a car together, and it was so funny. The guy selling it was so sketchy. He was some strange bald-headed, pudgy man who tried moving this piece-of-shit Honda on us.

"It's a great car. Everything is perfect, we can wrap it up now."

My brother didn't a say a single word to this man. He just took his scanner out of the car, surveyed the car, and then offered him $2,000 below the asking price. His logic was sound, and his offer was firm. The guy was not thrilled with it, and ultimately, we walked away from the deal.

Although that wasn't the car I ultimately got, it was nice to have the help of my little brother and to see him put his skills into action. We ultimately ended up getting a Subaru Outback, and he taught me how to make a few simple maintenance services to it. While I worked on my real estate license, he even brought me onto his job to do roadside service.

I found it so funny that I, of all people, would be doing roadside service. I know next to nothing about cars, but when I set my mind to something, I always close the gap. I'd like to think that it made my brother proud to see me step into his world a little and actually do well with it. It was a fun job, and it was rewarding to be able to help people when they needed it the most.

It was also beautiful working in the Hamptons and seeing the outstanding multi-million-dollar homes on Dune Road.

Being surrounded by beautiful and bright things always sparks my creativity and ambition. I also trusted that everything I was pouring into was just part of the path.

It actually led me to an interesting moment. I received a call from an older man that had a flat near the beach. When I found him, he was showing clear signs of heat exhaustion, and seemed disoriented. He drove a 1967 Chevy convertiable, and the tire had gone out on him, leaving him baking in the sun with the top down. At first, he was stubborn and didn't want to sit in my van, but when I saw him stand, his pants were sagging off of him, and he seemed like he was slurring his words. I pushed a little more, and he ultimately yielded and took a seat in the van. I gave him some water and got to work. I had never worked on a car like this before, so it took me a little bit to navigate it. He had a full-sized tire in trunk, and funny enough, it was his original spare tire. He told me that he had never changed the tires since he got the car. I was amazed that they held up that long, but after a short while, he was all set.

He mentioned to me that he was a vice chairman of a commercial real estate company, and I told him I had just earned my license.

Yes, you read that right, I got my license after finishing the 80-hour course and taking the exam. It was honestly really easy, but there was no time to celebrate. I was just moving from one objective to the next. Since I finished my license, I started working on my National Academy of Sports Medicine Certified Personal

Trainer test. My plan was to work in fitness and real estate. I started building my empire brick by brick.

The man, Rick, felt much better after I finished my work and insisted I follow him back to his house so he could give me a tip, show me some cool stuff, and pick my mind. He said that since I had helped him, he wanted to help me, too.

I followed him back, and he had a lovely property down a private road. It sat on the edge of the water. He told me that he went into commercial real estate years ago and never looked back. He was able to build the lifestyle he had on it by completely dedicating himself to the process.

In his garage, he showed me some beautiful classic cars that had been handed down the line of his family. He wrapped up our time by handing me a business card and insisting that we sit down together in the future to talk about real estate and other options.

After a short while, I would accept his offer to have a chat, but for the time being, I needed to keep charging ahead. Speaking of charge, I became a AAA-certified battery technician along the way, too. I then ripped through the NASM-CPT course load. It was a joke that I had to pay $2,000 to get a certificate that took me two weeks to earn, but alas, there is a cost to doing things the right way. I had considered going with ISSA, but at the last minute someone talked me out of it. I ultimately decided to use 1st Phorm as my standard and saw that everyone who was a leader in the company was a NASM trainer.

I swiftly pivoted into my next role and became the personal training director at a LA Fitness. Apparently, no one had ever been hired as a PTD directly before, so I ruffled some feathers with my arrival. Little did they know that the VP had immediately identified me as a replacement for him and said he could see me being VP in just a couple of months. This time was valuable in the cultivation of my sales skills. It was the first sales job I ever had, and I loved it. The hours were atrocious, and the pay was nowhere even close to what was told to me, but I still loved working in fitness and making a difference in the lives of people I came across.

After training under one of the other directors, I was ready to take my own location in Smithtown. When I walked in my first day, I told the sales associates that I had a goal of selling $30,000 in paid qualified invoice my first month. He immediately laughed at me and my lofty goal and said, "Good luck with that, buddy, we barely sold $2,000 last month."

I just smiled and thought to myself, "Well, of course you only sold that much—I wasn't here."

I just said, "You think I'm kidding, but I am dead serious. I have a plan, and I can definitely do it."

He scoffed at me again and just shrugged me off as naive at best.

However, I had the last laugh that month, as I sold more than $31,000 in PQI.

Of course, I had to give more than what was expected. That is just the kind of person I am. Also, to be fair, he quickly joined my team after I made my first five sales. Every time I closed another deal, he would come over, dap me up, and celebrate the win. I'd even get the perk of getting to go home a little early that day. Considering my days were 12 hours long, five days a week, plus a sick bonus half day on Saturdays, I was thrilled to say the least. Unfortunately, I was just not making anywhere close to the $10-$15,000 a month the VP had been boasting about to me when I signed. It was more like $3,500 and that was with being a top performer in my district. Fortunately, I had my first real estate deal in the works. I had found my mom and brother a home and was writing my first deal!

Everything was falling into place! I was about to make $9,000 from this deal and would be comfortable as I pushed into developing my training business and real estate portfolio.

Sike.

Although our initial offer was accepted, the seller's agent held another open house and received another offer $50,000 above the price we had offered.

We lost, I lost...

My heart broke as I told my mom the news that the deal fell through. She had been so proud to be buying her first home, and it *was a cute little spot by the water. However, with this wrench in our plans, my entire trajectory changed.*

Now we were being faced with an entirely new set of problems, as our lease was ending, and we had to move to another apartment in the next month. My plans of leaving in the next few months were shattered, and I knew what this future looked like. I think God decided that I still had work to do, and that I needed to suffer a little more to grow stronger.

As months of work and planning unraveled before me, I unraveled, too, but fortunately, I had the boys to help put me back together. I nearly broke. I was consumed by the failure, and I just didn't see a way ahead. I was broke, demoralized, and uncertain about my next move. However, the boys showed me that no matter what happened, they had my back and would help me push through.

I decided to take this time to slow down and reflect. I gave Rick a call, and we circled back to have a little discussion about the future. He invited me into his home, and I was inspired by the life he lived. I loved the books that lined his walls and the natural light that crawled through the windows. He told me to grab some gin and glasses before we went to sit on his patio. His garden was in bloom, and there were bright reds and yellows painting the bushes.

He poured me a drink, and my mind flashed to drinking gin with Jeff in Spain. It had been a little while since then. I don't even think I have had a drink since then.

"So, I read your book, and I really enjoyed it. I liked your story of overcoming hardship and learning how to forgive those who hurt you along the way," he said.

I recoiled slightly and felt a tear come to my eye. "Thank you for saying that. I am glad that you enjoyed the read. It was always a dream of mine to publish a book."

"Yes, yes, you are very sharp young man; however, the reason why I invited you over is because I want to talk about real estate. Tell me, what have you got going on now, and what do you want?"

I told him that since we last spoke, I took on a role as a personal training director, and my goal was to own a training business and to grow my real estate business.

He smiled a knowing smile, with a wisdom I came to respect. "It sounds like you are doing a lot of things, but my advice would be to choose just one."

Ah, this familiar adage once again crossing my path. I always felt that I had too many interests to just do one thing, and that I didn't want to limit myself.

"Look, I'm not saying abandon it, but maybe put one thing on the shelf for now. I could get you an interview at a commercial real estate firm tomorrow, no questions asked, and you'll probably get the job because you are an intelligent guy. However, what do you want? What does Ethan want?"

I paused. It was the first time I stopped in months, and I couldn't find my words.

"Well, that's a tough question. I want to do both, but I understand what you are saying. I have been told this many times in my life, but maybe now is the time to stop and consider the advice," I said.

He smiled at me and said, "I just want you to be happy because you saved my life. I really think you saved my life on that day, and I want to help. However, why don't we circle back to this when you know what you want for sure."

I left his home shortly after and thought deeply about what he said. I realized that real estate wasn't my passion; it was just a means to an end. I was trying to be successful at it so that I could live my passion. I realized that I was looking at it backwards. I need to dive into my passion to be successful, not the other way around.

I dug my hands into the earth again and planted new seeds. I made a resume and started searching for a solution to the cash flow problem. To call my resume a "resume" is an understatement; it is really more of a masterpiece, a work of art that always gets me the job I want. I also used my handy new friend, Chat GPT, to draft up some cover letters for each place I applied to until I finally got a bite.

My next move presented itself to me, and it was assistant manager position at a stretching facility. The opportunity looked great, and the owner described future regional opportunities to me. I felt that the core values of the company aligned with mine, and I loved being in the business of helping people feel better. I had a strong foundation of training, recovery, and anatomy already due to my own struggles of recovering from a car accident I was in. I put in my notice with LA Fitness and pivoted to my next objective. I saw a growth opportunity on the table for me with the pay I wanted and the autonomy to be a leader in the workplace. I flew to Fort Lauderdale, Florida, to do my training for the New York State Massage and Body Work Certificate, and I laughed at the fact I was called back to my old home.

Everything goes full circle, I suppose.

While there, I studied and mastered over 60 different stretches that linked in different protocols. It came easily to me, and I finished at the top of my class. While in town, I had the opportunity to swing by my storage unit to grab some of my belongings. I could squeeze about 50 lbs of things into my suitcase, and I ultimately had to abandon the rest. I knew when I was leaving that the odds of me being able to retrieve the rest were low at best, but I had not quite accepted the fact until later. I realized that this past year had been about growth and letting go of the past. That 10-by-10 unit was just a box full of anchors to a life I had outgrown and memories I no longer needed to cling to. Although I didn't realize it when I was there, I managed to surrender and just let go of those earthly attachments. They were just things, and I still had plenty of life ahead of me to live.

When I returned to NY, I was excited to start my new job, but it quickly devolved into a nightmare. My boss was an absolute dread to work with, and his understanding of leadership was quite different from mine. It ultimately became a place where I could not continue to suffer at, as it was draining my strength, and my hope for the future. That is about the nicest way I can describe that situation without getting into the details. My resignation ended with lengthy letter about the finer points of leadership and why his business would continue to suffer in the face of his mistreatment of employees. He countered with his own version of a "fuck you," and we split ways. I have walked away from bigger and better things, so this was barely a *stretch* for me to walk away from.

Look, no job is worth your sanity. I often tell my team that there is a difference between management and leadership, and that the former is the reason why most teams fail. When you are being micromanaged to the point where Big Brother is quite literally watching your every move and listening to your conversations, maybe it's time to go. If that is not enough to convince you, and if you are forced to endure a harangue of insults and disrespect from a disgruntled business owner, that would be your next sign to move on. You are a person; you deserve kindness, decorum, and the opportunity to grow.

I learned another valuable lesson, and it was to be specific about what I wanted. I decided that I wanted to be general manager at a kickboxing facility. It was important to me to have a high degree of autonomy and the ability to cultivate a team. I wanted the opportunity to progress into a regional role and eventually reach ownership.

After nights of searching online, I saw my chance: a job posting for general manager of a RockBox Kickboxing Arena. It was the right bone for this dog, so I sank my teeth into it. Just kidding, I'm not a dog at all; I was wolf entering the puppy pit, and I knew exactly how to outcompete and outmanuever all of my competition.

The next day, I called the facility directly and convinced the manager on duty that I was the best person for the job, and that if I had the opportunity to meet them in person, I would be able to prove that. I could feel him resonate with my passion and drive over the phone, and he said, "I believe you, man, you sound like the real deal. Come in here for a class."

I walked into the studio, convinced that the job was already mine, and that they just didn't know it yet. When taking the class, I laughed to myself at how perfect of an opportunity this was for me, because I knew I would excel here. I had been training in kickboxing every single day since I came back to the States. I started off the class pacing myself so as not to gas out. The trainer came up to me and tried correcting my form, so I had to turn the dial and show him what I was really made of.

I started slamming the bag with a flurry of round house kicks, front kicks, and spinning back kicks. When I locked eyes with him again, he did a little nod and acknowledged that he came over too soon. The manager on duty had seen me doing spinning back kicks and called me over as class ended.

"Dude, that was crazy. You are the real deal. You have some nasty kicks and are perfect for the job. I am going to set up a time for you to meet the owner," he said.

I further drove the point home and said, "Thank you for seeing that in me. I specifically looked for exactly this opportunity because I knew it would be the right environment for me. I transitioned careers this year because I knew that I was not living up to my full potential in accounting. I have experience managing dozens of bank accounts, reconciling millions of dollars, and cultivating people on my teams to be the best versions of themselves. I have relentlessly studied leadership for the past decade, and I am self-driven to excellence through my discipline. If I were given the opportunity to lead here, I will produce a top-performing team," I said.

He chuckled incredulously and said, "Bro, trust me, I think you are perfect. You have already convinced me, but let's set up this next call with the owner."

Later that week, I was called in again to sit with the owner, and I facetimed one of the original founders of the organization. I gave my pitch explaining why I was the man for the job. The owner asked me a question, and for the first time in any job interview, I didn't have to lie:

"Where do you see yourself in the next five years? Do you want to be a regional manager? Or maybe even ownership?"

I was stunned by the question and was so pleased that I could answer honestly, with the real truth:

"I have never seen myself as just an employee. I am far too ambitious to stay as an employee for the rest of my life, and I want a pathway to becoming a business owner. Right now, I am seeking growth, and I think that this is the perfect opportunity for me. I have been training in kickboxing every day, and I became a top performer in sales at both companies that I previously worked at. I am confident that if I was given the reigns, I cold lead our teams to success."

The founder took me in with a flat stare and said, "I can't tell if you are just a smooth talker or if you are the real deal, but brother, I'm willing to see what the truth is."

I told him, "Oh, I assure you I am the real deal, and the numbers won't lie."

Unfortunately, they couldn't offer me the general manager position to start because the posting was for a location that had not opened yet, so I started as an assistant manager at another location.

Fortunately, I blew it out of the water with my performance, and by happenstance, a general manager position opened after two weeks of grinding. I was quickly promoted into my next role. I also achieved an accolade of being the number-one salesperson in the country within our network in my first month of selling.

I was a hawk flying in the open sky. This was my element, and I refused to let anyone outperform me or compromise my next move to regional manager. My eyes were locked in on my target, and my driving thought was, "Oh, I am exactly who I said I was." Surely enough, in due time, I achieved that position as well.

I hired my new team and cultivated their talents. I told them that this would not be a job where I micromanage employees, and they dread coming in to work. Our culture here is simple: "We strive to be number one. I want you to work hard because there are opportunities for growth with your performance. There are many moving pieces right now, but if you show up and do the right thing, I will advocate for you every single time."

My location outperformed the others, and my initial team quickly progressed. After two months of cultivating them, building our relationships, and leading from the front, three of my original team members were identified as leaders and promoted to manager-level positions. My trainer was quickly recognized as one of the best in our region.

The key to it all? Treat people like people. Give them respect, courtesy, the grace to make a mistake, and the trust to perform their duties without micromanagement. When things didn't add up quite the way I expected, rather than going in guns blazing, I assumed one thing: "There is probably a good reason for this." The relief I feel as a leader with a highly competent team is that there, in fact, usually is a good reason. To the shock of most managers across America, people do indeed seem to perform better when given autonomy, trust, and the ability to solve a problem in more than one way. No two people are the same; therefore, people may come to different pathways of solving problems. However, I do not care what the mechanism is for solving a problem, so long as it is done correctly.

My performance was further recognized, and I became the main point of contact for training all our new sales associates because the results of my studio spoke for themselves.

At the end of it all, it feels like I started with a bobby pin and kept trading it up until I finally had a car. In the past year, I became a NYS realtor, an AAA-certified battery technician, and a NASM-CPT, and I earned my certification for massage and body work. I went from knowing nothing about sales to becoming a top performer, and I kept trading up my position for bigger and better roles.

There were times when I fell, and I wanted to stay on the ground, but I kept finding the strength to crawl to my feet and try again. When faced with failure or setbacks, people would voice their opinions and tell me, "You had your sabbatical of trying to make this work, but it is time to get realistic. You need to think about money, and you should think about going back to accounting."

In a weak moment, I even floated some of my resumes out and tried to convince myself that if I went back to accounting, I would go all in this time. I would study and get my CPA and just be the best accountant I could be. However, in the pit of my stomach, I knew I was just going back to what I thought was comfortable because I was afraid.

Fear is the dream killer; it tricks you into thinking that the things you want out of life are unrealistic and out of your reach. However, a wise man once wrote, "Whoever you are, or whatever it is that you do, when you really want something, it's because that desire originated in the soul of the universe. It's your mission on earth... and when you really want something, all the universe conspires to help you achieve it." – Paulo Coelho

In my heart, I know that this is true. I have reached into the soul of the world, and I saw that it was part of the soul of God, and that the soul of God was my own soul, and that I, a man, could produce miracles.

You are never too old to try again, friend. All that we have is today, and in any moment you choose, you can begin living the life you dream of. The lowest and most devastating moments of our lives can be the impetus of tremendous personal growth.

I have come to truly understand that life is talking to you. The pain you feel is from making decisions that are not aligned with your true heart, the one you are too scared to share with the world. The pain you feel is from trying to uphold the image of success versus the feeling of it.

True success in life comes from building meaningful relationships with those who you love and from doing work that you find meaningful.

I am constantly reminded that life is far too short. If not by the passing of those who I love, it is indicated by the gray hairs that sprout with increasing frequency.

Maybe you should stop putting the life you want to live on the backburner in place of the work you think you have to do to start enjoying life! Maybe you should enjoy life first, then find the work that you want to do?

People often confuse fear with logic. We are quick to write things off as impossible when the correct word would be "difficult."

Don't let the fear of the work stop you from starting your life's mission. Live courageously, take a leap of faith, and trust that you can weather any storm.

As I embark on this new chapter, I am reminded that life's greatest adventures await those courageous enough to pursue their dreams, no matter the obstacles they may face along the way. With faith as my compass and resilience as my guiding light, I march forward, ready to seize the boundless opportunities that lie ahead.

You, too, can produce miracles.

The Whispers of the Soul
A Collection of Poems

Hello again, my dear reader.

In the pages to come are some poems I wrote while I traveled. By no means am I the best poet in the world, but everyone has to start somewhere. I always found that writing in this style was therapeutic and helped me express my deeper emotions.

If it is a total flop, I understand, but hopefully you can find this enjoyable, too.

CLUTTER

In my late-night session of mental catch

I throw ideas off the walls of my cluttered
/ mind and see what bounces back

The thought of you pours through

A thought I'd rather not throw.

It may bounce back, but I'd rather not risk it.

Instead, I'll hold it close

Close to my heart

A thought held in a loving embrace

The only thought I'll keep to myself in this cluttered space.

TO ZERO

Sometimes
It is better
To start over

Break it all down
To zero
Take a new perspective.

Although it feels like
You lost everything
You haven't

Just remember
You keep all
Of what you learned

GROWTH

Humbled by the weight of adversity
I find my limits over and over again

Inspired by the fire in my soul
I rage beyond them again and again

Our growth stops
Only when we accept our limits

ROOTED IN LOVE

Empires of thought evaporated
Decades of planning abandoned

My world, burned to ashes
My heart lain to waste

Scorched by scorn and disillusion
Crushed by hands that were once gentle

From the ashes, all things must rise
All things die to be born again

The seeds of you planted in my mind
The idea of what could be

You've been growing not with vines, but roots
Anchoring in my heart

You wrap around me, pulling the pieces together
A tender embrace mending my wounds

Take root in my heart,
I want to see what sweet fruits you bear

Take root in me,
I will know each curve and groove

Take root in me,
I want to see your flowers bloom

Take root in me,
I want to take shelter in your shade

Take root in me,
so that I can love you

Thorns of Beauty

Women are like beautiful flowers
Great to look at, but all parts are toxic.

Things of beauty and violence.
Lacerating the hearts and souls of good men.

Men don't pick flowers because of the thorns.
The tighter you hold, the more it hurts.

Lie to yourself and say it will all be okay.
See the beauty that was once vibrant wilt and die.

No amount of water, sun, or love will
/ever help it heal. Let it die

UNYIELDING RESOLVE

The well has run dry
But I'll keep digging

When my tools break and fail me
I'll claw into the earth with bare hands

Scraping through layers of rock and dirt
I'll find what I'm looking for

There is an opportunity in suffering
A strength to be found

I'll dig beneath the bottom of the well
I'll dig into hell, and come back

You don't fucking know me

Threads of Light

Darkness is never all-consuming
There is always a single thread of light

I'll dig my hands into the earth
Pulling lightning out by the roots

I'll breathe deeply
Taking thunder in my lungs

With a roar and a slash
I will cut through the black veil

All storms pass, and this shall, too.

The Liberation of Tomorrow's Courage

Today is the day I kill myself

I can't go on living as the man I am
I can't go on living as a coward

With this death at my own hands
I will water the seeds in my ashes

With each death, and each incarnation
I come one lifetime closer to my truth

Today is the day I kill myself
So that tomorrow I can be brave

Unveiling of the True Self

Concentrate
Your attention
On a single point

Feed
Your intention
With your attention

Break
Your chains
Of the rusted past

Free
Your mind
Of the chains

Shape
Your body
Of your discipline

Become
Your embodiment
Of your true self

Embers of Transformation

An ember
Burning
Waiting for a life breath

A man
Working
Waiting for an opportunity

A mind
Sharpening
Waiting for the body

A body
Transforming
Waiting for the spirit

A spirit
Burning
Waiting for the man

VENOM

Crooked smiles
Teeth twisted by the lies behind them

Planting poison in your mind
Imitating empathy

Apex predator
Spider's web

Taking you in
Devouring you whole

OMENS

Your personal legend calls
The omens are whispering

Beyond the threshold of your fear
Is the boon of your courage

Released from your attachments
Step into the void

See the inner workings of your being
Turn into the wind

Forge of Ambition

Possessed by ambition
With these two hands
I will create
All that I envision

I will seize each opportunity buried in the dirt
I will grab firmly and pull it free from the earth

The world can be better
My community can be better
I can be better

All it takes is the sacrifice
Waste no energy
Fluid motions
Flow state

Break reality
And make it new
Break limitations
And be free.

TEMPERED STEEL

Unbroken blade
Drawn again
To vanquish demons

Hell's fury
Heaven's righteousness
Man's potential

Unsheathed
Grasped tightly
Decisive strike.

Quiet Ways of Saying "I Love You"

I don't believe in saying "I love you" anymore.
Not in the way that I used to say it, at least.

I don't want to be told by someone that they love me.
I want it to be shown to me.

Instead of saying "I love you" every night before bed
/ or in the morning before work.
Just don't say it.

Hold that feeling inside of you and find a way
/ to show each other how you feel.
Only on the most special of occasions
/ should you say "I love you"

Embracing the End of Suffering

At the edge of fear
Is bravery

At the edge of weakness
Is strength

At the edge of suffering

Is healing

At the edge of despair
Is hope

You choose the time
You choose when to begin

ETHOS IN ACTION

To have an impact
There must be gravity to your words

For your words to have any meaning
You must be the embodiment of your ethos

Hammer the words into your bones
Stoke the fire and burn away impurities

Walk with confidence, speak with authenticity
Become the philosophy you wish to teach

The Illusion of Constraint

Our minds can become prisons
When we choose to believe
We don't have a choice

That is the world's greatest lie
There is always a choice
You have your autonomy

Let go of that which doesn't serve you
Free your mind of scarcity and limitations
Open yourself to the abundance around you

There is always a choice
Choose wisely

A Soul's Tempest

It melts over broken bones
It fills the holes in shattered dreams

A flame that can never be extinguished
A storm that keeps raging

A blade that never rusts
A dream that never dies

My bones break, but my spirit remains

About the Author

- **NASM-certified personal trainer (NASM-CPT)**

- **Nationally certified in therapeutic massage and bodywork (NCBTMB)**

- **Licensed New York State realtor**

- **AAA-certified battery technician**

- **Bachelor of Science in Accounting (B.S. Accounting)**

Through the pages of his life's narrative, Ethan has woven a tapestry of resilience, self-discovery, and unwavering determination. His journey, etched with both triumphs and tribulations, serves as a testament to the human spirit's capacity to endure and transcend adversity.

Born into humble beginnings, he grappled with feelings of inadequacy and self-doubt from a young age. Yet instead of succumbing to the weight of these burdens, he forged ahead with an unyielding resolve to carve out his path to success.

Driven by an inner fire, he pursued personal excellence as his rebellion against the limitations imposed upon him. Each obstacle became an opportunity for growth, each setback a stepping stone toward his aspirations. Through introspection and self-reflection, he learned to navigate the tempests of life with grace and resilience.

His journey toward self-discovery led him to confront the demons within and to untangle the knots of anger and insecurity that bound him. Through meditation and introspective writing, he embarked on a journey inward, shedding the layers of doubt to reveal the core of his strength.

Today, Ethan stands as a beacon of hope and inspiration, a testament to the transformative power of perseverance and self-belief. His words resonate with authenticity and depth, offering solace to those navigating their own storms and guiding them toward the light of self-acceptance and inner peace.

The Ink of My Soul and the Fire in My Bones, Second Edition

ISBN Paperback: 978-1-63765-432-3

The Ink of My Soul and the Fire in My Bones is a thoughtful and vividly descriptive story depicting a young man's battle with his quarter-life crisis. The story begins with a sense of urgency and panic as Ethan realizes he is about to graduate from college with a degree but finds no joy in his work. He questions what happened to his passion and starts reflecting on his most intimate memories and experiences to understand how he reached this point. While sifting through his feelings, he is confronted with the deep emotional trauma of his past. He comes to realize that his current sense of identity has been limited by unwittingly allowing events from his past to define him. When he gathers the courage to confront the aspects of himself that he once felt ashamed of, he discovers the strength to forgive both himself and those who have hurt him.

The author possesses a unique voice that blends elements from poetry, philosophy, and personal enrichment books. He sidesteps the typical clichés of personal development by allowing readers to draw their own conclusions about life, rather than rigidly outlining another 'thirty-two step plan to be a millionaire by the time you are thirty-two' kind of book. His narratives immerse the reader deep into the landscape of his mind and initiate a conversation about change.

www.ingramcontent.com/pod-product-compliance
Lightning Source LLC
Chambersburg PA
CBHW071655160426
43195CB00012B/1473